2022 / 2023

EVENTDESIGN JAHRBUCH
EVENT DESIGN YEARBOOK

2022 / 2023

EVENTDESIGN JAHRBUCH
EVENT DESIGN YEARBOOK

Katharina Stein

avedition

EINE BRANCHE IM LERNPROZESS
AN INDUSTRY IN A LEARNING PROCESS 6
Introduction by Katharina Stein

AUF DER SUCHE
NACH NEUEN ERLEBNISSEN
IN SEARCH OF NEW EXPERIENCES 8
Interview with Betty Schimmelpfennig, Elastique.

PUBLIC

Journey of the Pioneers 16
ATELIER BRÜCKNER for Dubai Future Foundation

IAA MOBILITY 2021 22
Atelier Markgraph, jangled nerves for Mercedes-Benz

Cheer up Stuttgart Initiative 28
Designplus for Designplus

G-Class X Matrix Resurrections World Premiere 32
Oliver Schrott Kommunikation for Mercedes-Benz

Der erste landesweite Katastrophenschutztag NRW 36
EREIGNISHAUS for Ministry of Internal Affairs
of the state of North Rhine-Westphalia

Esch2022 Remix Opening 40
Battle Royal for Esch2022 European Capital of Culture

TÜBKE MONUMENTAL 46
KUNSTKRAFTWERK Leipzig
for KUNSTKRAFTWERK Leipzig

Tiny Window Concerts 52
KULTUR KIOSK Sara Dahme for KULTUR KIOSK

RosinenBAR THF 56
die wellenmaschine for die wellenmaschine

KI-Konferenz 60
facts and fiction for Federal Ministry of Labour
and Social Affairs (BMAS) /
Policy Lab Digital, Work and Society

unzeen Gaming Studio Concept 64
MIKS for unzeen Investorengemeinschaft
Jakob Braendle

MITTENDRIN 68
SceneDeluxe – Andrea Bohacz for KulturFunke Lübeck*

2021 EQS China Road Show 72
Uniplan for Mercedes-EQ

Jasmina Jovy Jewelry Showroom Prevent 78
Steffen Vetterle, Jasmina Jovy Jewelry for
Jasmina Jovy Jewelry

Culture Lab @CAMPUS GERMANY 82
VOSS+FISCHER for Federal Ministry for
Economic Affairs and Climate Action

PARTNERS

Vodafone Kick-offs 2021 88
insglück for Vodafone

Hendrick's Grand Hotel 92
Proof & Sons, zwanzigzwanzig for
William Grant & Sons Brands

eBay Open 2020.digital 96
insglück for eBay

Bayer Capital Markets Meeting 100
onliveline for Bayer

FRIENDS

got2b Make-up Launch Event 106
STAGG & FRIENDS for Henkel

The Sphere of Amazing 110
insglück for Supreme Committee for
Delivery & Legacy (SC)

Dachser – General Leadership Meeting 2021 114
onliveline for Dachser

The Unconventional Experience –
A Brand onboarding 118
STAGG & FRIENDS for Active Nutrition
International | Powerbar

Countdown Clock Launch 122
fischerAppelt, live marketing for Supreme Committee
for Delivery & Legacy (SC)

INHALT
CONTENTS

PRESS

beyerdynamic Pro X Launch Event   *128*
Bruce B., 0711 Livecom for beyerdynamic

THE LÄND Press Conference Umbrella Brand Event   *132*
*MILLA & PARTNER, Jung von Matt NECKAR
for State Ministry Baden-Württemberg*

Mercedes-Benz Pre-Night IAA 2021   *136*
Oliver Schrott Kommunikation for Mercedes-Benz

EMPLOYEES

C:onference 1.21 – Time to transform   *142*
MUTABOR for CARIAD

Fujitsu Employee CEE Kick-off 21   *146*
HEAD OF EVENT for Fujitsu Technology Solutions

Mercedes-Benz Global Training Experience Citan 21   *150*
*STAGG & FRIENDS for Mercedes-Benz
Global Training*

EUNited 2021   *154*
Uniplan for Michelin Reifenwerke

EXPERTS

Signals of Hope   *160*
fischerAppelt, live marketing for Frankfurter Buchmesse

SAP NOW Germany   *164*
insglück for SAP Deutschland

Open up new Dimensions – Hybrid Oncology Launch   *168*
onliveline for Daiichi Sankyo Europe

Marc Cain Fashion Film "Keep on Dancing"
Spring / Summer 2022   *172*
Marc Cain for Marc Cain

eleVation DIGITAL DAYS   *176*
Uniplan for Vodafone

HHS – Hamburg Hemophilia Symposium   *180*
onliveline for Takeda Pharma Vertrieb

JUNG Loves ... Exhibition of Things   *184*
raumkontor for Albrecht Jung

GROHE X Experience Hub   *188*
VOK DAMS for Grohe

OPPO Find X3 Series Global Launch   *192*
Uniplan for OPPO Mobile Telecommunications

BSS LogiStream   *196*
Kreativ Konzept for BSS Bohnenberg

STUDENT PROJECTS

Schlemmer X Beats   *202*
*Studioproduktion Event Media HdM for
Staatsgalerie Stuttgart*

Dachmobil   *208*
*DHBW Ravensburg for Landesinnungsverband des
Dachdeckerhandwerks Baden-Württemberg*

Graduation Celebration 2021   *212*
*TH Deggendorf Master Students of Media Technology
for University administration / Alumni network*

Plantasia   *216*
*Studioproduktion Event Media HdM
for Zentrum für Sonnen- und Wasserstoffenergie (ZSW)*

ZWISCHEN ANSTURM UND PERSONALMANGEL
BETWEEN RUSH DEMAND AND A LACK OF PERSONNEL   *220*
Interview with Uta Goretzky, IFES

IMPRESSUM
IMPRINT   *222*

ayscan *In den digitalen Raum mit ayscan: Unter
www.ayscan.de herunterladen, den
Anweisungen folgen und die mit Symbol versehenen Seiten um
Bild, Film und Ton erweitern. Viel Spaß! Enter digital space with
ayscan: Download at www.ayscan.de, follow the instructions and
scan pages marked with the symbol to enjoy additional photos,
films and sounds. Have fun!*

Nach über zwei Jahren mit COVID-19 scheint mittlerweile ein helles Licht am Ende des Tunnels. Eine Mehrheit der Menschen ist mehrmals geimpft und im Frühjahr 2022 wurden viele Corona-Auflagen zurückgenommen. Die meisten Events können wieder stattfinden!

Doch die Freude ist getrübt. Nach der Pandemie folgt ein neues Problem: der akute Personalmangel. Besonders Konzertveranstalter:innen, aber auch Agenturen sind betroffen. Damit wird „nicht nur Material [...] knapp und teuer, Gleiches gilt auch für die wichtigste Ressource Mensch", so Uta Goretzky, IFES Executive Director (Seite 220). Die einzige Lösung: Die Arbeitsverhältnisse müssen endlich attraktiver werden.

Hinzu kommt der grausame Krieg in der Ukraine, der die bereits aufgewühlte Welt mit einer weiteren Katastrophe auf die Probe stellt. Geradezu wohltuend ist es da zu sehen, wie viele Menschen (und auch die Veranstaltungsbranche) keinen Moment zögern, sich solidarisch zu zeigen, Spenden zu sammeln und im Rahmen der Möglichkeiten zu helfen.

TROTZ ABKLINGENDER PANDEMIE UND ÜBERALL SPÜRBARER FREUDE ÜBER JEDES EVENT, LEICHT GESTALTET SICH DER NEUSTART DER BRANCHE NICHT!

Dabei hat sich vieles getan: Die Offenheit für neue Ideen und Technologien hat enorm zugenommen. Neue Formate und Ansätze haben sich professionalisiert. Die Verflechtung mit anderen Branchen war und ist ein großer Gewinn, das hat auch Betty Schimmelpfennig, Managing Partner von Elastique. (Seite 8) so erlebt. Wir haben viele wertvolle Erfahrungen gesammelt.

Doch 2021 gab es im Vergleich zum Vorjahr keine richtig großen Weiterentwicklungen. Schon nach dem ersten Pandemiejahr wurde zu Recht betont, dass wir uns am Anfang der Entwicklungen befinden. Und dort sind wir immer noch. Ein ganzes Stück weiter, aber eben immer noch mitten im Lernprozess.

Neben vielen Lerneffekten gibt es auch Fragen, auf die wir bis jetzt keine guten Antworten haben. So lassen sich Events mit einem informativen und co-kreativen Charakter gut digital abbilden. Emotionale und atmosphärische Bestandteile dagegen sind schwer zu vermitteln. Auch die viel beschworenen hybriden Events sind alles andere als gut entwickelt. Wie genau digitale und analoge Gäste zielführend miteinander verwoben werden können, wie man jeweils zum Medium passende Erlebnisse schafft und zugleich ein Gemeinschaftsgefühl erzeugt, das wissen wir derzeit noch nicht.

Eine Perspektive weist uns ein neues, wenn auch überstrapaziertes Thema: das Metaverse. Noch sind wir weit entfernt von einem der Definition nach „richtigen" Metaverse. Doch dem Konzept ähnliche virtuelle Erlebniswelten oder Online-Spiele, in denen wir als Avatare an Konferenzen teilnehmen, shoppen gehen oder spielerische Räume erkunden, zeigen uns neue Möglichkeiten und Chancen digitaler Erlebnisse auf.

Viele bisherige Entwicklungen und auch einige Projekte in dieser Ausgabe lassen interessante Ansätze erkennen, in manchen Punkten aber noch keine ganzheitlich betrachtet idealen Antworten. Das ist auch völlig in Ordnung. Zum jetzigen Zeitpunkt geht es primär um eines: möglichst aktiv am Lernprozess teilzuhaben!

In diesem Sinne viel Freude beim Stöbern, Einordnen und Lernen.

EINE BRANCHE IM LERNPROZESS
AN INDUSTRY IN A LEARNING PROCESS
INTRODUCTION BY KATHARINA STEIN

After over two years with COVID-19, there is now a bright light at the end of the tunnel. The majority of people have had multiple vaccines and in spring 2022 many corona measures were eased. Most events can take place again!

However, this joyful mood is marred by a new problem following the pandemic: the acute lack of personnel, affecting concert organisers in particular but also agencies. "Not only is material scarce and expensive, the same applies to the people as the most important resource", says Uta Goretzky, IFES Executive Director (page 220). The only solution: working conditions must finally become more attractive.

In addition, there is the gruesome war in the Ukraine, which is putting the world that is already in turmoil to the test with yet another catastrophe. It is pleasing to see how many people (including the event industry) are not hesitating for a moment to show solidarity, collect donations and help within the realms of the possible.

DESPITE THE WANING PANDEMIC AND THE PALPABLE DELIGHT ABOUT EVERY EVENT, THE RESTART OF THE INDUSTRY IS NOT PROVING EASY!

A lot has been set in motion, however: openness to new ideas and technologies has significantly increased. New formats and approaches have been professionalised. The interweaving with other sectors was and is a big advantage, as is also experienced by Betty Schimmelpfennig, Managing Partner of Elastique (page 8). We have gathered a wealth of valuable experience.

But in 2021 there was not any great further development compared to the previous year. It was emphasised rightly after the first pandemic year already that we were at the start of developments. And we are still there now. Progress has been made but we are still in the midst of a learning process.

Apart from a lot to learn, there are also questions to which we do still not have any good answers. Events with an informative and co-creative character can be represented well digitally. Emotional and atmospheric aspects, on the other hand, are difficult to convey. And the highly eulogised hybrid events are everything other than well developed. We currently still do not know how exactly digital and analogue guests can be interlinked purposefully with each other, how to create experiences suitable for the respective medium and at the same time generate a community feeling.

One perspective shows us a new albeit overworked topic: the metaverse. We are still far away from a "proper" metaverse in terms of definition. But virtual experience worlds or online games similar to the concept, in which we take part in conferences as avatars, go shopping or explore playful spaces show us new possibilities and opportunities of digital experiences.

Many previous developments and also some of the projects featured in this edition reveal interesting approaches but in some respects still no ideal overall answers. And that is quite alright. At the current point in time, it is primarily about one thing: participating as actively as possible in the learning process!

In this spirit, enjoy browsing, evaluating and learning.

Bei Elastique. beschäftigt ihr euch schon lange mit den Schnittstellen unserer analogen und digitalen Realität. Die Pandemie hat hier vieles in Gang gesetzt. Wie hast du als thematisch erfahrene Kreative die Zeit erlebt? Hat sie dir neue Ansätze und Konzepte eröffnet?

Auch wenn es für viele Branchen leider eine sehr bittere und harte Zeit war und wir auch nicht wirklich wussten, wie es für Elastique. laufen würde, haben rückwirkend betrachtet viele Unternehmen sehr wichtige Erfahrungen gemacht. Die Dynamik und der Veränderungswille, die sich in vielen Ebenen der Wirtschaft gezeigt haben, waren beeindruckend. Es wurde lösungsorientiert daran gearbeitet, die Krise zu bezwingen und im Idealfall sogar gestärkt daraus hervorzugehen.

Dabei wurden Konzepte, die beispielsweise in der TV-Branche bewährt sind, auf den Design- und Kommunikationsbereich übertragen. Plötzlich gab es überall digitale Keynotes, die für ihre innovative Machart hoch gelobt wurden. Dabei musste man manches Mal ehrlich sagen, dass es sich im weitesten Sinne um klassische TV-Formate handelt, die man auf den Bereich der Marken- und Produktkommunikation übertragen hat.

Spannend wurde es, als diese Formate mit neuen Technologien wie den XR-Stages kombiniert wurden, was wir selber an mehreren Projekten ausloten durften.

Mich lehrt es, dass wir uns viel häufiger branchenübergreifend austauschen und umschauen sollten – denn durch den Einsatz eigentlich gut bekannter Prinzipien in anderen Kontexten kann immer wieder wirklich Neues entstehen – und dies kann Branchen verändern!

Was hast du generell aus den letzten zwei Jahren gelernt? Welche neuen Möglichkeiten haben sich entwickelt und etabliert – und werden uns auch in Zukunft weiterbringen?

Wir arbeiten bei Elastique. schon von jeher kollaborativ und interdisziplinär – die stärkere Verlagerung unseres Kreationsprozesses in den digitalen Raum hat unserem Ansatz nochmals mehr Schub gegeben.

Da hatten wir dann plötzlich mitten in der Pandemie drei neue Mitarbeitende in Berlin, die wir erst Monate später physisch kennenlernen durften – dennoch sind wir in unserer Kultur verbunden. Jetzt sind es schon fünf Berliner:innen und es ist ein Elastique.-Berlin-Hub daraus entstanden. Wie ich finde, eine wirklich schöne Entwicklung!

Auch in der Arbeit mit Studierenden konnte ich einen großen Paradigmenwechsel beobachten – habe ich doch meine Professur in Wiesbaden während der Pandemie und rein digital angetreten. Dabei wurde mir klar:

MANCHE KREATIONSPROZESSE SIND REIN DIGITAL INITIIERT DEUTLICH EFFEKTIVER, SCHNELLER UND „VERBUNDENER" ZU REALISIEREN.

Die Ergebnisse lassen sich merklich besser dokumentieren als an analogen Post-it-Wänden, und diese digitale Arbeitsweise gibt den Studierenden oder Teams viel mehr Möglichkeiten, mit den Ergebnissen weiterzuarbeiten. Das ist eine gute Erkenntnis und ein Gewinn – aber letztlich sind ein persönlicher Austausch, ein echtes Gespräch, eine reale Diskussion durch kein digitales Tool zu ersetzen.

Zukünftig wird es also immer mehr darauf ankommen, verschiedene Ansätze und digital/analoge Arbeitsweisen geschickt zu kombinieren, um inspirierende und innovative Kreationen zu tätigen und dabei auch sinnstiftend im Team zusammenarbeiten zu können.

Ein großes Thema sind sogenannte hybride Formate. Wirklich viele oder gute Lösungen, analoge und digitale Teilnehmende tatsächlich miteinander zu verbinden, gibt es aber noch nicht. Wie könnte das deiner Meinung nach zukünftig aussehen?

AUF DER SUCHE NACH NEUEN ERLEBNISSEN
IN SEARCH OF NEW EXPERIENCES
INTERVIEW WITH BETTY SCHIMMELPFENNIG, ELASTIQUE.

At Elastique. you have been interested for a long time in where our analogue and digital realities overlap. The pandemic has set a lot in motion here. How have you experienced this time as a creative mind with experience in this field? Has it opened up new approaches and concepts for you?

Even if it has unfortunately been a very bitter and tough time for many sectors and we did not really know how it would go for Elastique., looking back many companies have gathered important experiences. The dynamism and the willingness to change that have been evident on many levels in the economy have been impressive. There has been solution-orientated work towards overcoming the crisis and ideally even emerging from it stronger than ever.

Concepts that have been tried and tested for example in the TV industry have been transferred to the field of design and communication. Suddenly there were digital keynotes everywhere that have been highly praised for their innovative style. Sometimes one had to say honestly that these were classical TV formats in the widest sense that were applied to the field of brand and product communication.

It became interesting when these formats were combined with new technologies such as the XR stages, which we were able to try out ourselves on several projects.

What it has taught me is that we ought to communicate and look around much more often across different sectors – because by applying principles that are well-known in other contexts, novelties can often emerge – and this can change industries!

What have you learnt in general from the last two years? What new possibilities have developed and established themselves – and will continue to bring progress in future?

At Elastique. our work has always been collaborative and interdisciplinary – the increased shift in our creation process towards digital space has given our approach a further boost.

In the midst of the pandemic, we suddenly had three new employees in Berlin, who we were only able to physically meet in person months later – even so, we are united by our culture. Now there are already five people in Berlin and an Elastique. Berlin hub has been formed. I find this is really a welcome development!

I was also able to observe a big paradigm shift in the work with students – given that I started my professorship in Wiesbaden during the pandemic and on a purely digital basis. It became clear to me:

SOME CREATION PROCESSES THAT ARE INITIATED PURELY DIGITALLY CAN INDEED BE REALISED MORE EFFECTIVELY, QUICKER AND MORE "COHERENTLY".

The results can be documented noticeably better than on analogue post-it walls and this digital way of working gives the students or teams a lot more possibilities of further work on the results. This is a positive finding and an advantage – but ultimately personal interaction, true conversation, a real discussion cannot be replaced by any digital tool.

In future it will therefore increasingly be about combining a variety of approaches and digital/analogue work methods in a clever way, in order to realise inspiring and innovative creations and to be able to work meaningfully within a team.

So-called hybrid formats are a big topic. However, there are still not many or no good solutions for actually combining analogue and digital participants. How could this develop in future, in your opinion?

Was wir nach der Pandemie vor allem durch Events und Treffen physischer Art merken: Das rein Digitale wird die Realität nie ersetzen. Wir sind Lebewesen aus Fleisch und Blut und brauchen den Kontakt zu anderen Menschen. Physisch und direkt. Schon um die Jahrtausendwende gab es Versuche, physischen Stimulus mit Anzügen und Sensoren skurrilster Art zu übertragen – es wirkte immer wie eine Krücke. Diese prinzipiellen Rahmenbedingungen gelten heute noch.

Ich glaube, die emotionale Qualität digitaler Zusammenkünfte wird sich erst dann signifikant steigern, wenn sie unmittelbar wird – also nicht über Brückentechnologien läuft, sondern direkt an unsere Sinne gebunden ist. Langfristig vielleicht über Technologien wie Neuralink, egal ob man solche Entwicklungen befürwortet oder nicht.

Doch bis dahin wird sich das Publikum hybrider Events wohl weiterhin aus zwei Gruppen zusammensetzen: diejenigen, die froh sind, das Geschehen live vor Ort erleben zu können, und diejenigen, die „zugeschaltet" sind und eher intellektuell durch die vermittelten Inhalte und Interaktionsmöglichkeiten reagieren.

Manche sagen, dass wir uns bei Online-Erlebnissen an dem orientieren müssen, was online funktioniert: Derzeit sind das Games. Werden künftige digitale Erlebnisse in diese Richtung gehen?

Ich denke, wir sollten generell möglichst viel aus anderen Bereichen lernen und auf Online-Erlebnisse aus dem Kommunikationsbereich übertragen.

Es gibt aber auch über die Jahre hinweg immer wiederkehrende Zyklen: Als wir mit Elastique. gestartet sind, wurden maximal viele Online-Erlebnisse als sogenannte „Webspecials" extrem spielerisch gestaltet. Damit haben wir in den ersten Jahren unser Geld verdient. Bei der Kommunikation von Marken und Produkten stand das Erlebnis ausdrücklich im Vordergrund – vieles war mit Bewegtbild, Sound und Game-Mechaniken angereichert.

Danach kam allerdings eine Zeit, in der man sich nicht mehr durch komplizierte Storys klicken wollte, um an Informationen zu gelangen. Alles wurde „flat" und extrem

„accessible". Schnörkellose Informationen. Mit der Öffnung der Game-Technologien von Unity bis Unreal durch WebGL Exporter oder die Pixelstreaming-Technologie schlägt das Pendel nun wieder in die andere Richtung – man will durchaus wieder digital „erleben".

WORAUF ES BEI DIGITALEN ERLEBNISSEN ANKOMMT: DIE ART DER INTERAKTIONEN SOLLTE PRÄZISE GEWÄHLT SEIN.

Viel zu oft läuft man in der Marken- und Produktkommunikation durch irgendwelche Metaverses, in denen man zu relativ interaktionslosen Besucher:innen verdammt wird, die höchstens herumlaufen und sich Dinge anschauen können. Vielleicht darf man auch ein wenig miteinander chatten oder Tanzmoves ausführen.

Das kann und sollte es aber nicht sein! Denn da müssen wir Gestalter:innen uns zum einen mit der Gaming-Industrie messen. Zum anderen sollten die Interaktionskonzepte ganz präzise so entwickelt werden, dass sie perfekt zu den Inhalten passen, die wir vermitteln wollen.

Und wie viel spannender wird es, wenn wir völlig ungesehene Interaktionen erschaffen, bei denen wir digital interagieren, aber dabei mit der physischen Welt in Kontakt treten, in der sich unsere Interaktionen manifestieren! Und andersherum.

Kannst du ein Beispiel beschreiben, wie die Verbindung von digitalen und physischen Welten aussehen könnte?

Wir haben 2021 gemeinsam mit The Game und Journee ein Teilprojekt für BMW bei der IAA realisiert. BMW hatte zu der Zeit sein Metaverse „Joytopia" gelauncht. Unsere Idee war es, eine Brücke zwischen dem physischen Space

What we have realised after the pandemic, especially through events and meetings of a physical nature, is that the purely digital will never replace reality. We are human beings of flesh and blood and need contact with other people. Physical and direct. Around the turn of the millennium there were attempts to replicate a physical stimulus with the most bizarre suits and sensors – it always acted as a crutch. These principal framework conditions still apply today.

I think that the emotional quality of digital gatherings will only really rise when they become direct – so not running through bridge technologies but appealing directly to our senses. In the long term, perhaps by means of technologies such as Neuralink, regardless of whether one is in favour of such developments or not.

But until then, the public for hybrid events will no doubt continue to comprise two groups: those who are happy to have the chance to experience the events live on site and those who are "tuned in" and react in a more intellectual manner to the content and interaction possibilities being conveyed.

Some say that when it comes to online experiences, we must orientate ourselves to what works online: at the moment that is games. Will future digital experiences go in this direction?

I think that in general we should learn as much as possible from other industries and apply this to online experiences in the field of communication.

However, over the years there are recurring cycles: when we started with Elastique., as many online experiences as possible were designed extremely playfully as so-called "web specials". We earnt our money with this in the initial years. When communicating brands and products, the experience was explicitly in the foreground – many aspects were enriched with moving images, sound and game mechanics.

But after that there came a time when one no longer wanted to click through complicated stories to get to information. Everything became "flat" and extremely "accessible". Straightforward information. With the launch of game technologies from Unity to Unreal through WebGL Exporter or pixel streaming technology, the tide is now turning again – there is once again a wish to "experience" digitally.

WHAT IS IMPORTANT FOR DIGITAL EXPERIENCES: THE TYPE OF INTER-ACTION SHOULD BE CAREFULLY SELECTED.

Far too often in brand and product communication, one runs through some or other metaverses in which one is condemned to visitors with relatively little interaction, who at the most can rush around looking at things. Perhaps they may chat with each other a little or carry out dance moves. But this is not how it could or should be! We the designers must on the one hand pit ourselves against the gaming industry in this. On the other hand, the interaction concepts should be developed precisely so that they perfectly match the content we want to convey.

And it gets even more interesting if we create fully novel interaction in which we interact digitally but come into contact with the physical world where our interactions manifest! And vice versa.

Can you describe an example of how the combination of digital and physical worlds might look?

In 2021, we realised a partial project for BMW at IAA together with The Game and Journee. BMW had launched its metaverse "Joytopia" at the time. Our idea was to build a bridge between the physical space of BMW at Max-Joseph-Platz in Munich and the metaverse. Concretely: What if I could reach into the metaverse with my hand and it became visible on the "other side" for digital participants from around the world – who would be present there as avatars?

von BMW am Max-Joseph-Platz in München und dem Metaverse zu bauen. Konkret: Was wäre, wenn ich mit meiner Hand in das Metaverse hineingreifen könnte und die Hand auf der „anderen Seite" für die digitalen Teilnehmer:innen aus aller Welt – die dort als Avatare präsent wären – sichtbar würde?

Genau das haben wir umgesetzt. So konnte man als Besucher:in via Leap Motion Sensor mit der eigenen Hand als eine Art „Hand of God" das Metaverse beeinflussen. Auf der digitalen Seite wurde die Hand zu einer Wolke, aus der man Objekte wie Blitze, Regenbögen, Brezeln, Fischschwärme oder Partikel auf die Avatare im Metaverse herunterrieseln lassen konnte. Zeitgleich konnten Besucher:innen des Metaverse die Person in München sehen, wie sie ihre Hand in den Ring hält.

Was so einfach klingt, war technologisch eine große Herausforderung. Letztlich hat es aber funktioniert und alle hatten großen Spaß an dieser Verbindung der zwei Welten. Die Möglichkeiten dieses „Merge" werden wir in zukünftigen Projekten noch weiter ausloten!

Du hast es gerade schon angesprochen. Ein anderes, aktuelles Hype-Thema ist das Metaverse. Was denkst du darüber und wird es sich diesmal durchsetzen können?

Der Begriff ist meines Erachtens aktuell ein wenig überstrapaziert. Ich glaube schon, dass sich die Qualität unserer digitalen Erlebnisse und unsere Beziehung zu digitalem „Besitz" signifikant verändern werden. Schauen wir uns doch Kinder an, die von Erlebnissen in Roblox – nichts anderes als ein schon voll funktionales und höchst lebendiges Metaverse – so erzählen, als hätten sie diese in der „analogen Welt" erlebt. Oder wie wichtig es vielen ist, welche Kleidung ihr Avatar in den verschiedensten Anwendungen trägt.

Was noch vor wenigen Jahren belächelt wurde, wird jetzt „gefühlt", spielt für viele Menschen tatsächlich eine große Rolle.

ENTSCHEIDEND IST, DASS WIR AUS VERGANGENEN VERSUCHEN LERNEN UND WIRKLICH NEUE ERLEBNISSE SCHAFFEN.

Viel zu wenig wird von den Erfahrungen in „Second Life" berichtet – das ja schon damals daran scheiterte, dass keine funktionierenden Lösungen für übergriffige digitale Interaktionen oder Pornografie gefunden wurden. Denselben Problemen sieht sich nun Meta ausgesetzt und diskutiert daher „Safe Zones".

Das zeigt: Die Ansätze sind nicht neu. Aber nun könnte ihre Zeit gekommen sein, weil Digitalität für uns viel selbstverständlicher geworden ist.

Noch spannender finde ich die immer stärkere Verankerung unserer physischen Welt in der digitalen Sphäre. Durch die Blockchains mit Tokens wie NFTs werden viele Besitztümer und Daten im digitalen Raum festgeschrieben. Ich persönlich glaube, dass diese Prinzipen unsere Realität in den kommenden Jahren noch deutlich mehr prägen werden als das Metaverse.

Betty Schimmelpfennig ist Co-Founder und Managing Partner bei Elastique. und Professorin für Crossmediale Gestaltung an der Hochschule RheinMain.

www.elastique.de
www.hs-rm.de/de/hochschule/personen/
schimmelpfennig-betty

That is exactly what we realised. As a visitor, one could influence the metaverse with one's own hand via Leap Motion as a kind of "hand of god". On the digital side, the hand became a cloud from which objects such as lightning, rainbows, pretzels, swarms of fish or particles could rain down onto the avatars in the metaverse. At the same time, visitors to the metaverse could see the person in Munich holding their hand in the ring.

What sounds so simple was a great technical challenge. But in the end it worked and everyone had great fun with this connection between two worlds. We will sound out the possibilities of this "merge" further in future projects!

You have just touched on the metaverse as another current hype topic. What do you think about it and will it be able to establish itself this time?

In my opinion, the term is currently a little overstretched. I do think that the quality of our digital experiences and our relationship to this digital "asset" will change significantly. Just take a look at children who talk about experiences on Roblox – nothing other than an already fully functional and highly animate metaverse – as if they had experienced them in the "analogue world". Or how important it is to some people what clothes their avatar is wearing in various applications.

What was still laughed at a few years ago is now "felt", actually plays a big role for many people.

WHAT IS DECI-SIVE IS THAT WE LEARN FROM PREVIOUS ATTEMPTS AND CREATE TRULY NOVEL EXPERIENCES.

Much too little is reported about the experiences in "Second Life" – which failed already back then because no functioning solutions were found for molesting digital interactions or pornography. Meta is now facing the same problems and is therefore discussing "safe zones".

This shows: he approaches are not new. But now their time may have come, because digitality has become much more par for the course for us.

I find the increasing anchoring of our physical world in the digital sphere even more interesting. Through the block chains with tokens such as NFTs, many assets and data are rooted in digital space. I personally believe that these principles will shape our reality significantly more in forthcoming years than the metaverse.

Foto: @aboycalled7daysisaweekend

Betty Schimmelpfennig is co-founder and Managing Partner at Elastique. and Professor of Cross-media Design at RheinMain University.

www.elastique.de
www.hs-rm.de/de/hochschule/personen/
schimmelpfennig-betty

Jede Zielgruppe hat unterschiedliche Bedürfnisse und Erwartungen. Dementsprechend sind Eventkonzepte im Idealfall nicht nur auf den Absender, sondern vor allem auf die Empfänger zugeschnitten.

PUBLIC: EINE BREITE ÖFFENT-LICHKEIT, DIE SICH AUS EINWOHNERN, TOURISTEN, PASSANTEN, FLANEUREN ETC. ZUFÄLLIG ZUSAMMENSETZT. DEMENTSPRECHEND HETEROGEN – IN (SOZIALER) HERKUNFT, ALTER ODER VORLIEBEN – ZEIGT SICH DIESE ZIELGRUPPE, DIE NICHT NUR SEHR GROSS, SONDERN IN DER ANSPRACHE NICHT EINDEUTIG ZU FASSEN IST. WAS DEN JEWEILIGEN PERSONEN ALLERDINGS GEMEIN IST, IST EIN NICHT KOMMERZIELLES INTERESSE.

Each target group has different requirements and expectations. Event concepts are therefore ideally not only geared towards the addressor, but especially towards the recipients.

PUBLIC: A WIDER PUBLIC IS COMPOSED BY CHANCE OF INHABITANTS, TOURISTS, PASSERS-BY ETC. THIS TARGET GROUP IS HETEROGENEOUS ACCORDINGLY – IN TERMS OF (SOCIAL) BACKGROUND, AGE OR PREFERENCES – AND IS NOT ONLY VERY LARGE, BUT ALSO DIFFICULT TO GRASP IN TERMS OF APPEAL. HOWEVER, WHAT THESE PEOPLE HAVE IN COMMON IS A NON-COMMERCIAL INTEREST.

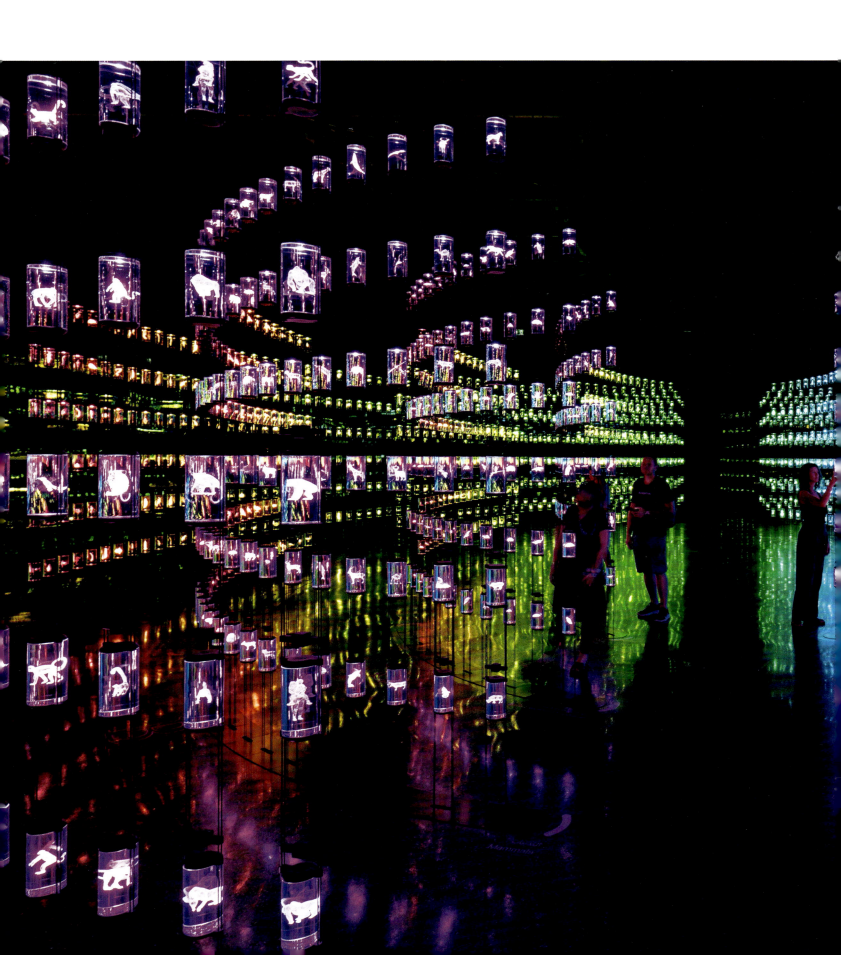

JOURNEY OF THE PIONEERS
ATELIER BRÜCKNER, STUTTGART

Location
Museum of the Future, Dubai

Client
Dubai Future Foundation, Dubai

Month / Year
February 2022 (Launch)

Duration
Permanent

Dramaturgy / Direction / Coordination
ATELIER BRÜCKNER, Stuttgart

Architecture
Killa Design, Dubai

Lighting
BELZNER HOLMES, Stuttgart

Media
medienprojekt p2, Stuttgart
(Hardware planning)

Others
Buro Happold, Bath (MEP and Structural design); OSS HOPE: AltSpace, Limassol (Arrival window, Earth overview); Galerija 12+, Belgrade (Orientation, Monument to the pioneers, Recruitment, Application stations); Framestore, London (Take-off, Return); HEAL INSTITUTE: Galerija 12+, Belgrade (The Window); Marshmallow Laser Feast, London (The Garden, The Forest, The Lab); Certain Measures, Berlin (The Observatory); Superflux, London (The Library); ALWAHA: Deeplocal, Pittsburgh / Emilie Baltz, New York (Movement therapy, Feel therapy, Connection therapy); Polytope Agency, Los Angeles (Grounding therapy, Sound design entrance); Jason Bruges Studio, London (The Centre)

Photos
Giovanni Emilio Galanello, Milan; Daniel Stauch, Stuttgart (Exterior view)

Das Museum of the Future ist seit Februar 2022 die neueste Attraktion Dubais. Von außen zieht allein die ikonische und ungewöhnliche Architektur von Killa Design die Aufmerksamkeit auf sich. Im Innern erwartet die Besucher:innen ein von ATELIER BRÜCKNER gestaltetes ganzheitliches Erlebnis.

The Museum of the Future has been the latest attraction in Dubai since February 2022. The iconic and unusual architecture by Killa Design draws attention from the outside in itself. In the interior, an immersive experience designed by ATELIER BRÜCKNER awaits visitors.

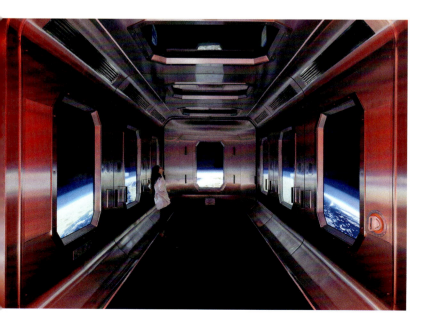

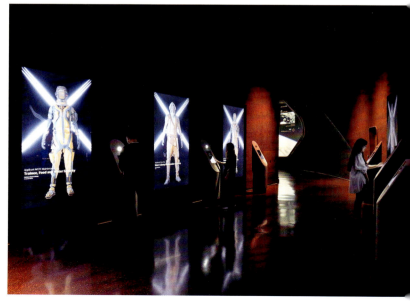

STARKE RAUM-BILDER UND IMMERSIVE INSTALLA-TIONEN SCHAFFEN EIN AUSSERGEWÖHN-LICHES GESAMT-ERLEBNIS.

Die Ausstellung „Journey of the Pioneers" ist über drei Etagen und 3000 Quadratmeter Ausstellungsfläche hinweg als immersives Erlebnis gestaltet. Jede Etage ist gleich einem filmischen Setting mit starken Raumbildern angelegt und fokussiert eine Vision der Zukunft: Leben im Weltraum, Bioengineering und Regeneration geschädigter Ökosysteme sowie individuelles Wohlbefinden.

The exhibition "Journey of the Pioneers" is set up over three floors and 3000 square metres of exhibition space. Each floor is like a film setting with striking scenography, focussing on a vision of the future: life in space, bioengineering and the regeneration of damaged ecosystems, as well as individual wellbeing.

STRIKING SCENOGRAPHY AND IMMERSIVE INSTALLATIONS CREATE AN EXCEPTIONAL IMMERSIVE EXPERIENCE.

Beispielsweise soll der mystische Raum „The Library" die Vielfalt und Schönheit der Flora und Fauna vermitteln. 2400 von der Decke hängende Glaszylinder mit eingravierten Arten sind als begehbare Rauminstallation angeordnet und faszinieren mit dem Detailreichtum der Natur.

For example, the mystical space "The Library" is designed to convey the variety and beauty of the flora and fauna. 2400 glass jars with engraved species hanging from the ceiling are arranged as a walk-in installation and fascinate with their wealth of details of nature.

Die choreografierte Raumfolge, Klang und Duft entreißen die Teilnehmenden dem Alltag und lassen sie in eine greifbare futuristische Welt eintauchen. Lichtführung und Materialwahl tragen entscheidend zum sinnlichen Erlebnis bei. So entstammen etwa die Wände der Raumstation einem 3D-Drucker und scheinen aus extraterrestrischem Material gefertigt zu sein. Die Wände des HEAL Institute sind aus nachhaltigem Karuun, gewonnen aus der Rattanpalme. Das Material Lehm ist im Ausstellungsbereich ALWAHA raumbildend eingesetzt. Jedes Detail ist präzise formuliert und hat seine Bedeutung für den Gesamteindruck und die Aussage.

The choreographed sequence of spaces, sounds and fragrances takes participants away from everyday life and allows them to immerse themselves in a tangible futuristic world. The lighting design and choice of materials contribute significantly to the sensory experience. The walls of the space station, for instance, were created using a 3D printer and appear to be composed of an extraterrestrial material. The walls of the HEAL Institute are made of sustainable karuun, extracted from the rattan palm. The material loam is used to shape the space in the ALWAHA exhibition area. Every detail is precisely formulated and plays a role in the overall impression and the message.

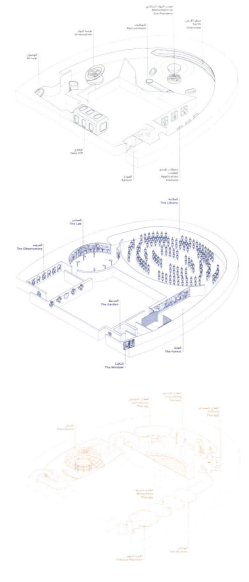

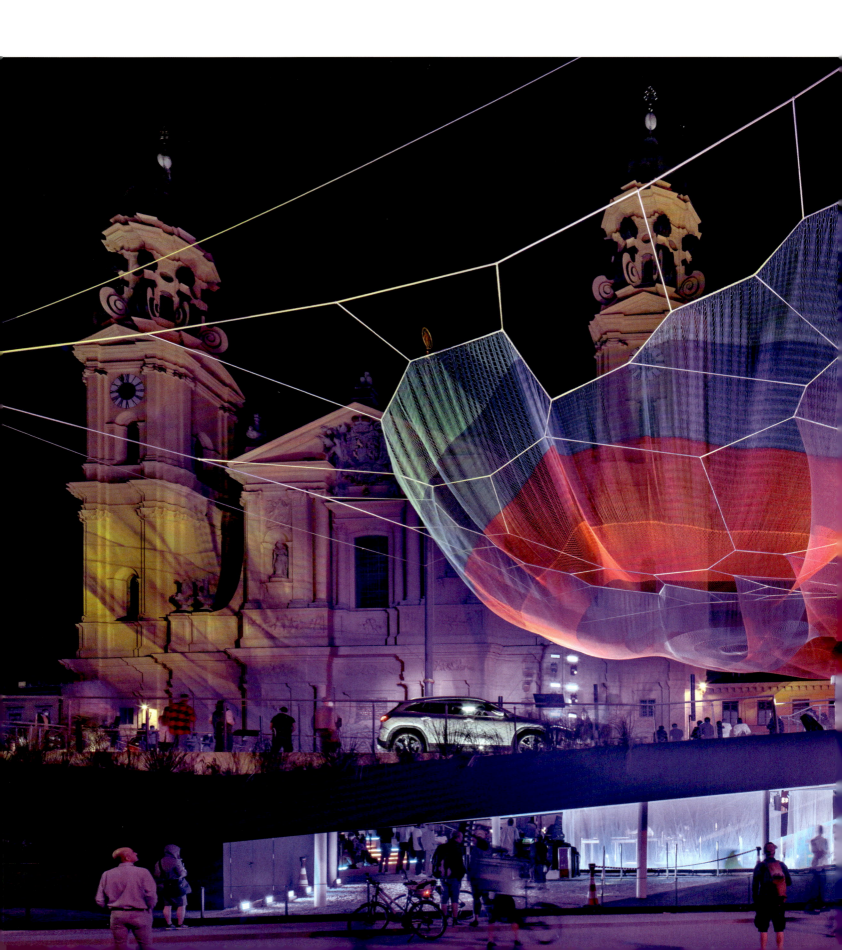

IAA MOBILITY 2021
ATELIER MARKGRAPH GMBH, FRANKFURT AM MAIN; JANGLED NERVES GMBH, STUTTGART

Location
Odeonsplatz, Munich

Client
Mercedes-Benz AG, Stuttgart

Month / Year
September 2021

Duration
6 days

Dramaturgy
Atelier Markgraph GmbH, Frankfurt am Main (Communication, Staging)

Architecture / Design
jangled nerves GmbH, Stuttgart

Music
Brandt Brauer Frick; Rival Consoles; Lisa Morgenstern; Stimming × Lambert; Hania Rani

Photos
Andreas Keller, Altdorf; Kristof Lemp, Darmstadt; Copterbrothers / jangled nerves, Stuttgart (Drone picture)

Mercedes-Benz präsentierte sich anlässlich der IAA MOBI-LITY 2021 mit einer kostenfreien, öffentlichen Markenfläche auf dem Odeonsplatz in München. Eingebettet zwischen historischen Gebäuden bot der zweistöckige Bau einen Platz für Kultur, Kunst und die Präsentation von E-Mobilität.

EINE MARKEN-INSZENIERUNG ZUR IAA 21 WIRD ZUM ÖFFENTLICHEN UND KULTURELLEN ERLEBNISRAUM.

A BRAND PRESENTATION FOR IAA 21 BECOMES A PUBLIC AND CULTURAL EXPERIENCE.

On the occasion of IAA MOBILITY 2021, Mercedes-Benz presented itself with a free of charge, public brand space on the Odeonsplatz in Munich. The two-storey platform nestled among historical buildings offered a showcase for culture, art and the presentation of e-mobility.

Das begehbare, begrünte Dach war der Startpunkt für
die Besuchenden. Es war Aussichtsplattform wie Verweil-
und Flaniermeile und informierte mit analogen Exponaten
über die Nachhaltigkeitsziele der Marke. Die in der Mitte
geknickte Plattform schuf unter sich zwei Teilräume, die für
die Markenpräsentation genutzt wurden. Apps boten als
digitale Verlängerung weitere Informationen rund um Produkte und Services.

The walkable, planted roof was the starting point for visitors,
as a viewing platform and as a strolling promenade with
analogue exhibits providing information about the sustainability goals of the brand. The platform, being kinked in the
middle, formed two separate areas that were used for the
brand presentation. Apps offered further information about
the products and services as a digital extension.

Der Bau war mit einer 24 mal 21 Meter großen, schwebenden Kunstskulptur von Janet Echelman überspannt. Unter dem Namen „*Earthtime 1.26 Munich* – presented by Mercedes-Benz" symbolisierte das Netz unser vernetztes Ökosystem. Bei Dunkelheit ließen Lichtinszenierungen die Skulptur wie ein organisches Gebilde erscheinen.

A large, floating art sculpture measuring 24 by 21 metres by Janet Echelman spanned the building. Under the name *"Earthtime 1.26 Munich* – presented by Mercedes-Benz", the net symbolised our networked ecosystem. In the dark, the lighting design gave the sculpture the appearance of an organic entity.

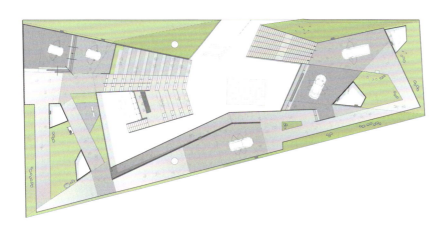

Am Abend wandelte sich die die Markenfläche zu einer Musikbühne und lud zur Konzertreihe „Artificial Soul presented by Mercedes-Benz" ein. Mit den Klängen der neoklassischen Künstler:innen Brandt Brauer Frick, Rival Consoles, Lisa Morgenstern, Stimming × Lambert, Hania Rani und den Lichtinszenierungen über und auf der Medienfläche entstand ein faszinierendes Zusammenspiel mit Erlebnischarakter.

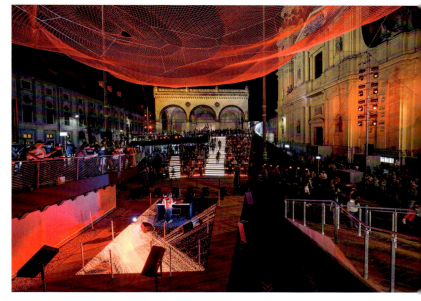

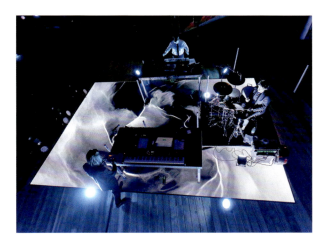

The brand space was transformed into a music stage in the evening, inviting visitors to a series of concerts called "Artificial Soul presented by Mercedes-Benz". A fascinating interplay and rich experience were created by the sounds of the neoclassical artists Brandt Brauer Frick, Rival Consoles, Lisa Morgenstern, Stimming × Lambert and Hania Rani, together with the lighting design above and on the media display.

CHEER UP STUTTGART INITIATIVE
DESIGNPLUS GMBH, STUTTGART

Location
Stores and public places, Stuttgart

Client
Designplus GmbH, Stuttgart

Month / Year
2021

Duration
Several months

Dramaturgy / Direction / Coordination / Architecture / Design
Designplus GmbH, Stuttgart

Participants
ave anziehsachen; Bloody Colors Tattoo Studio; Café Kaiserbau, Condesa, Da Vinci Engineering, L. A. Signorina (Marienplatz); Jakob Conceptstore; Kallas; KLEINER DØNNER (Hairdresser); Landesmuseum Württemberg / Die Dürnitz (Altes Schloss); MR Design Studio; Optik Martin; Sattlerei; still thrifting | vintage shop; Studio HANS / vitra. by storeS; Werbewelt; ZÜBLIN car park / KULTUR KIOSK

Photos
Designplus GmbH, Stuttgart

Um während der Pandemie zu verdeutlichen, wie wichtig der Einzelhandel, die Gastronomie, die Kunst- und Kulturstätten sowie all ihre Protagonisten für unser Miteinander sind, initiierte Designplus eine installative Aktion. Im Juni 2021 tauchten bis zu drei Meter große aufblasbare Smileys an wechselnden Orten in Schaufenstern oder an öffentlichen Plätzen in der Stuttgarter Innenstadt auf.

In order to highlight during the pandemic how important retailing, gastronomy, art and culture venues and all their protagonists are for our society, Designplus initiated an installation campaign. In June 2021, inflatable smileys up to three metres in size appeared in alternating locations, on shop windows or on public squares in the city centre of Stuttgart.

MEHR VERBUNDENHEIT DURCH DAS WOMÖGLICH BEKANNTESTE LÄCHELN UNSERER ZEIT.

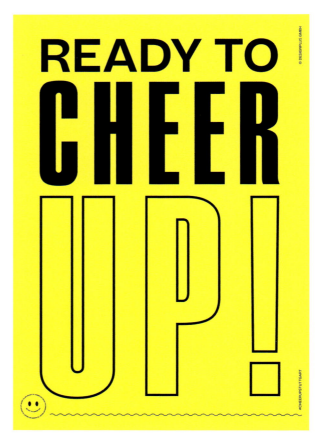

MORE TOGETHER-NESS THROUGH ONE OF THE MOST FAMILIAR SMILES OF OUR TIMES.

Ähnlich dem Regenbogensymbol, das im ersten Lockdown weltweit ein Zeichen für Solidarität und Optimismus verbreitete, sollten die überdimensionalen Smileys auf die besonders unter dem Lockdown leidenden Geschäfte und Orte aufmerksam machen. Mit einem Lächeln und stets wechselnden Locations haben sie Mut, Inspiration und eine positive Stimmung versprüht und zugleich mit einem Augenzwinkern und Leichtigkeit eine Verbindung zu den Menschen hergestellt.

Die Aktion wurde medial auf allen Kanälen von Designplus und den teilnehmenden Partnern unter dem Hashtag #cheerupstuttgart verbreitet. Begleitend wurden Aufkleber und Plakate in der Stadt verteilt. 2022 soll die Reise der Smileys fortgesetzt werden.

Similar to the rainbow symbol that spread solidarity and optimism worldwide during the first lockdown, the oversized smileys were intended to draw attention to the shops and localities that suffered particularly under lockdown measures. With a smile and constantly changing locations, they exuded courage, inspiration and a positive mood, whilst at the same time forging a connection to people with a wink and lightheartedness.

The campaign was broadcast on all the media channels of Designplus and the participating partners under the hashtag #cheerupstuttgart. Stickers and posters were distributed in the city alongside this. The journey of the smileys is set to continue in 2022.

G-CLASS X MATRIX RESURRECTIONS WORLD PREMIERE

OLIVER SCHROTT KOMMUNIKATION GMBH, COLOGNE

Location
Castro Theater, San Francisco

Client
Mercedes-Benz AG, Stuttgart

Month / Year
December 2021

Duration
1 day

Dramaturgy / Direction / Coordination / Architecture / Design / Graphics / Lighting / Media / Films
Oliver Schrott Kommunikation GmbH, Cologne

Music
Artlist.de

Artists / Show acts / Construction
Plastique Fantastique, Berlin

Photos
*Plastique Fantastique, Berlin;
Daniel Camino, Köln*

EINE ÜBERGROSSE INSZENIERUNG MIT STARKEM PR- UND SOCIAL-MEDIA-EFFEKT.

A powerful idea with a PR effect was to be developed on behalf of Mercedes-Benz for the world film premiere of "Matrix: Resurrections", as an extension of the brand cooperation between the automobile manufacturer and film production. OSK took up the theme of the red pill for this, which has great significance in the Matrix film series and stands for freedom and courage.

Im Auftrag von Mercedes-Benz sollte für die Film-Welt-premiere von „Matrix: Resurrections" eine starke Idee mit PR-Effekt entwickelt werden. Eine Verlängerung der Markenkooperation zwischen Automobilhersteller und Filmproduktion. OSK griff dafür die rote Pille auf, die in der Matrix-Filmreihe eine große Bedeutung hat und für Freiheit und Wagnis steht.

Das Ergebnis war eine Aufsehen erregende Inszenierung, die die Gäste schon vor der Ankunft am roten Teppich begrüßte: Auf der Straße direkt vor dem Castro Theatre in San Francisco setzte die Agentur einen G-Klasse-Geländewagen in einer riesigen roten Pille in Szene. Die Inszenierung verknüpfte zentrale Elemente des Films mit dem Produkt Mercedes-Benz G-Klasse. Neben der roten Pille nimmt auch der grau lackierte Geländewagen mit dem Stern eine wichtige Rolle im Film ein.

Bauliche Unterstützung erhielt die Agentur vom Künstlerduo Plastique Fantastique. Die Berliner Künstler:innen konstruierten die 12 Meter lange und 3,50 Meter hohe Installation aus dem Kunststoff Polyurethan. Das Material ist transparent und gleichzeitig sehr farbintensiv. Vor Ort wurde die Pille mit Nebel gefüllt, was den Showcharakter des Settings zusätzlich betonte. Anschließend ging das Objekt als Selfie-Backdrop auf Social-Media-Plattformen um die Welt.

A LARGE-SCALE STAGING WITH A POWERFUL PR AND SOCIAL MEDIA EFFECT.

The result was a sensational staging that welcomed guests already before their arrival on the red carpet: On the street right in front of the Castro Theatre in San Francisco, the agency set the scene for a G-Class SUV in a giant red pill. The setting brought together central elements of the film and the Mercedes-Benz G-Class product. Apart from the red pill, the grey SUV with a star also plays an important role in the film.

The agency received constructional support from the artist duo Plastique Fantastique. The Berlin artists built the 12-metre-long and 3.5-metre-high installation out of the plastic polyurethane, a material that is transparent and at the same time rich in colour. The pill was filled on site with mist, which additionally emphasised the show character of the setting. The object subsequently went around the world on social media platforms as a selfie backdrop.

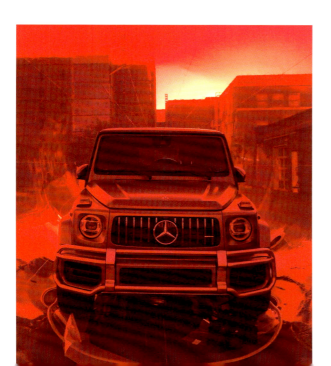

DER ERSTE LANDESWEITE KATASTROPHENSCHUTZTAG NRW
EREIGNISHAUS AGENTUR FÜR LIVE-MARKETING, COLOGNE

Location
Münsterplatz, Bonn

Client
Ministry of Internal Affairs of the state of
North Rhine-Westphalia, Dusseldorf

Month / Year
October 2021

Duration
1 day

Dramaturgy / Direction / Coordination
EREIGNISHAUS – Agentur für
Live-Marketing, Cologne

Architecture / Design / Media
EREIGNISHAUS – Agentur für
Live-Marketing, Cologne; Kopfkunst – Agentur
für Kommunikation GmbH, Münster

Graphics / Text
Kopfkunst – Agentur für Kommunikation
GmbH, Münster

Lighting / Technology
Presentation Service Kurt Breuers
GmbH, Neuss

Films
Bernd MSC Schroers Medienproduktion,
Cologne; EREIGNISHAUS – Agentur für
Live-Marketing, Cologne

Music
Jazz Choir Bonn

Artists / Show acts
Shary Reeves (Moderator); Springmaus
Improvisationstheater, Cologne

Decoration
Profil & Design GmbH, Bad Honnef;
Roschdeko, Niederkassel

Catering
STREET-KITCHEN Catering & Events,
Cologne

Construction
JP Mobile Spaces GmbH, Hamburg (incl.
Temporary constructions action course)

Others
UP Werbemittel, Münster (Promotional mate-
rials); Media-e-Motion Thorsten Borchers,
Neuss (Live streaming, Landing page)

Photos
Pixty Fotografie Reza Daioleslami, Cologne

On behalf of the Ministry of Internal Affairs of the state of North Rhine-Westphalia, as well as the seven major aid organisations for disaster prevention, EREIGNISHAUS set up and managed the first state-wide disaster prevention day NRW on Münsterplatz in Bonn. Based on the example of a power cut, the task was to inform the people and the active disaster management team and to strengthen their ability to help themselves.

NRW'S FIRST DISASTER PREVENTION DAY – WITH INTERACTIVE INFORMATION AND A VARIETY OF LIVE EVENTS.

Im Auftrag des Ministeriums des Innern des Landes Nordrhein-Westfalen sowie den sieben großen Hilfsorganisationen im Katastrophenschutz konzipierte und leitete EREIGNISHAUS den ersten landesweiten Katastrophenschutztag NRW auf dem Münsterplatz in Bonn. Die Aufgabe bestand darin, am Beispiel eines Stromausfalls die Bevölkerung sowie die aktiven Katastrophenschützer:innen zu informieren und die Selbsthilfefähigkeit zu stärken.

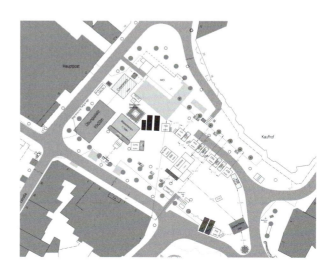

DER ERSTE KATASTROPHEN-SCHUTZTAG NRW – MIT INTERAKTIVEN INFORMATIONEN UND VIELSEITIGEN LIVE-AKTIONEN.

Unter der Leitidee „BLACKOUT – Was geht, wenn nichts mehr geht?" wurde ein abwechslungsreiches Programm entwickelt. Die BLACKBOX, eine interaktive Ausstellung in schwarz folierten Schiffscontainern, bildete das Herzstück. Dort konnten sich Besuchende informieren und mit dem BLACKCHECK Informations-Sammelkarten mitnehmen.

A varied programme was developed in accordance with the guiding idea "BLACKOUT – what works when nothing is working?" The BLACKBOX, an interactive exhibition in ship containers decked with black foil, formed the centrepiece. Visitors could find out more there and collect the BLACK-CHECK information cards to take with them.

Live-Aktionen wie eine organisationsübergreifende Übung sowie verschiedene Talkrunden gaben einen Eindruck vom Alltag und Teamgeist der ehrenamtlichen Katastrophen-schützer. Auftritte von Künstler:innen und Musiker:innen unter der Moderation von Shary Reeves rundeten das Geschehen familienorientiert ab. Eine Landingpage bot die Livestream-Übertragung des Bühnenprogramms, begleitet von einem BLACKOUT-QUIZ. Zusammen mit der Agentur Kopfkunst wurde ein Mediakonzept mit Funkspots, Plakatie-rungen, Edgarcards sowie Bewegtbild-Content und Social-Media-Postings umgesetzt.

Live events such as a drill across all the organisations and various rounds of talks conveyed an impression of the everyday lives and team spirit of the disaster prevention volunteers. Performances by artists and musicians, moderated by Shary Reeves, rounded off the event on a family-orientated note. A landing page provided the livestream transmission of the stage programme, accompanied by a BLACKOUT QUIZ. A media concept was realised together with the agency Kopfkunst, comprising radio spots, billposting, Edgar cards, moving image content and social media posts.

ESCH2022 REMIX OPENING
BATTLE ROYAL GMBH, BERLIN

Location
Esch-sur-Alzette City; Esch-Belval

Client
Esch2022 European Capital of Culture,
Esch-sur-Alzette

Month / Year
February 2022

Duration
1 day

Dramaturgy
Battle Royal GmbH, Berlin; Les Enfants
Terribles Theatre Company Ltd, Reigate

Direction / Coordination
Battle Royal GmbH, Berlin

Architecture / Design / Graphics
Battle Royal GmbH, Berlin; Holla Creative
Outsourcing, Yeovil

Lighting
Chris Moylan Optikalusion, Berlin

Media
Duncan McDade for Battle Royal GmbH,
Berlin (Lead motion design) / Maxin10sity,
Budapest; Andreas Schindler, Berlin;
Basil Hogios, Prague; Pixway GmbH,
Berlin; InFocusAV, Lancaster

Music
Basil Hogios, Prague

Decoration / Fitting
Battle Royal GmbH, Berlin; Hinnerup
Productions ApS, Hvidovre

Construction
adhoc engineering GmbH, Potsdam / apex
Luxembourg; PRG Germany, Hamburg;
MAGNUM France, Gonesse; Stageco Belgi-
um N. V., Tildonkbelgium; The Powershop
Belgium BV, Werchter; Lunatx Special Effects
GmbH, Dusseldorf

Others
Denis We & Team, Berlin (Choreography);
SATURN Production, Berlin (Health
and safety); Freecaster / Broadcasting Center
Europe, Luxemburg (Broadcasting)

Photos
Kooné, Berlin; Paul Gärtner, Karlsruhe;
Chris Moylan Optikalusion, Berlin

Im Februar 2022 fand der offizielle Start der europäischen Kulturhauptstadt Esch2022 statt. Unter dem Motto REMIX FUTURE entwickelte Battle Royal Studios einen unkonventionellen Eröffnungsabend. Er sollte die Menschen aus der lokalen Gemeinde zusammenbringen und so über das Kulturjahr hinaus eine kulturelle Identität stiften und langfristig stärken.

Das Event wurde als komplexe Reise im Stil einer geheimen Mission ausgestaltet. Durch Lösen von Rätseln und das gemeinsame Erzeugen sogenannter Co-Creation Energy für die Region waren die Gäste die treibende Kraft hinter dem Erlebnis. Höhepunkt des Abends war der Start von Augmented-Reality-Raketen, die von mehr als 800 Schüler:innen als Teil eines Malwettbewerbs eingereicht worden waren – mit dem gemeinsamen Ziel, die Zukunft zu „remixen".

EINE ERÖFFNUNGS-FEIER, DIE DIE REGION, IHRE MEN-SCHEN UND DEREN BETEILIGUNG IN DEN FOKUS STELLT.

AN OPENING CERE-MONY WITH A FOCUS ON THE REGION, ITS PEOPLE AND THEIR PARTICIPATION.

The official launch of the European Capital of Culture Esch2022 took place in February 2022. Under the motto of REMIX FUTURE, Battle Royal Studios developed an unconventional opening ceremony. It was designed to bring people from local communities together and thereby to forge and reinforce a cultural identity in the long term beyond the cultural year.

The event was designed as a complex journey in the style of a secret mission. The guests were the driving force behind the experience, by solving puzzles and participating in generating so-called co-creation energy for the region. The highlight of the evening was the launching of augmented reality rockets, which had been submitted by more than 800 pupils as part of an art competition – with the common goal of "remixing" the future.

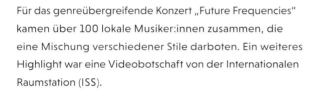

Für das genreübergreifende Konzert „Future Frequencies"
kamen über 100 lokale Musiker:innen zusammen, die
eine Mischung verschiedener Stile darboten. Ein weiteres
Highlight war eine Videobotschaft von der Internationalen
Raumstation (ISS).

Over 100 local musicians came together for the concert
entitled "Future Frequencies", presenting a mix of different
genres and styles. A further highlight was a video message
from the International Space Station (ISS).

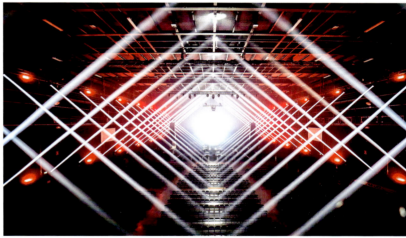

Public participation was the focus of the event – both online and offline. A show narrated in parallel across two main stages carried the evening, while visitors embarked on an eventful scavenger hunt on site, supported by 200 volunteers. Surveys and live interaction tools incorporated digital viewers online.

Im Fokus des Events stand die Publikumsbeteiligung – sowohl on- als auch offline. Eine über zwei Hauptbühnen parallel erzählte Show trug den Abend, während sich die Besucher:innen vor Ort auf eine erlebnisreiche Schnitzeljagd begaben, unterstützt von 200 Volunteers. Online banden Umfragen und Live-Interaktionstools die digital Zuschauenden ein.

Live-Musik, DJ-Sets, Tanzperformances, Videomappings, Lichtinstallationen und eine breite Palette immersiver Interaktionen brachten die Stadt zum Leben. Unter COVID-konformen Bedingungen wurden zirka 18.000 Gäste vor Ort und 14.000 weitere online begrüßt.

Live music, DJ sets, dance performances, videomappings, light installations and a wide range of immersive activations brought the region to life. Under conditions that complied with COVID regulations, around 18,000 guests were welcomed on site and a further 14,000 online.

TÜBKE MONUMENTAL
KUNSTKRAFTWERK LEIPZIG GMBH, LEIPZIG;
FRANZ FISCHNALLER

Location
KUNSTKRAFTWERK Leipzig

Client
*KUNSTKRAFTWERK Leipzig GmbH,
Leipzig*

Month / Year
March – December 2022

Duration
9 1/2 months

Dramaturgy
*Franz Fischnaller (Artistic &
Technical direction)*

Direction / Coordination
*KUNSTKRAFTWERK Leipzig
Markus Löffler (Initiator, Producer and
Organiser)*

Art direction / Graphics
*Franz Fischnaller with Cineca VisitLab
and DIAC*

**Digitalisation and interactive platform
(Tübke Touch)**
Centrica srl

Music
Steve Bryson (Music and Composition)

Sponsorship
*Ostdeutsche Sparkassenstiftung
with Sparkasse Leipzig and a Leipzig civic
initiative*

In Cooperation with
*Leipzig Trail Art; Panorama Museum Bad
Frankenhausen; HTWK Leipzig*

Photos
Luca Migliore

Neueste Technologien schaffen nicht nur außergewöhnliche Bilder, sie bieten auch neue Vermittlungsansätze und Kunst-Erfahrungen. Ein Beispiel dafür ist TÜBKE MONUMENTAL, ein vielgestaltiges Projekt, das bis zum 31. Dezember 2022 im KUNSTKRAFTWERK in Leipzig präsentiert wird. Die immersive Multimedia-Installation ist eine Hommage an den Maler Werner Tübke (1929–2004), Mitbegründer der Leipziger Schule und Schöpfer des Bauernkriegspanoramas „Frühbürgerliche Revolution in Deutschland" (1983/87). Mit einer Größe von 4 mal 123 Metern ist es eines der größten Gemälde Mitteleuropas.

ONE OF THE BIGGEST PAINTINGS IN CENTRAL EUROPE CAN BE RESEARCHED DIGITALLY AS A MULTIMEDIA INSTALLATION.

The latest technologies not only create exceptional images, they also offer new approaches to mediation and art experiences. An example of this is TÜBKE MONUMENTAL, a multifaceted project that is being presented until 31 December 2022 at KUNSTKRAFTWERK in Leipzig. The immersive multimedia installation is a homage to the painter Werner Tübke (1929–2004), co-founder of the Leipzig School and creator of the Peasants' War panorama "Early Bourgeois Revolution in Germany" (1983/87). With a size of 4 by 123 metres, it is one of the biggest paintings in Central Europe.

EINES DER GRÖSSTEN GEMÄLDE MITTELEUROPAS WIRD ALS MULTIMEDIAINSTALLATION DIGITAL ERFORSCHBAR.

Anlässlich des 90. Geburtstags des Malers im Jahr 2019 beschlossen Markus Löffler, Direktor des KUNSTKRAFTWERK, und der New-Media-Künstler Franz Fischnaller, das imposante Gemälde in die digitale Welt zu transformieren.

Die Multimedia-Installation THE GREAT CIRCLE ist eine Komposition Fischnallers aus zwölf Szenen des Panoramabildes. In Kooperation mit Cineca entwickelte er daraus ein Skript und konzipierte dynamische 3D-Modelle. Diese werden in einer 27-minütigen Präsentation von 25 Projektoren in einer Auflösung von 21.840 mal 2000 Pixeln auf die 1200 Quadratmeter große Fläche der Maschinenhalle übertragen und durch Soundeffekte von Steve Bryson untermalt.

On the occasion of the 90th birthday of the painter in the year 2019, Markus Löffler, Director of KUNSTKRAFTWERK, and the new media artist Franz Fischnaller decided to transfer the imposing painting to the digital world.

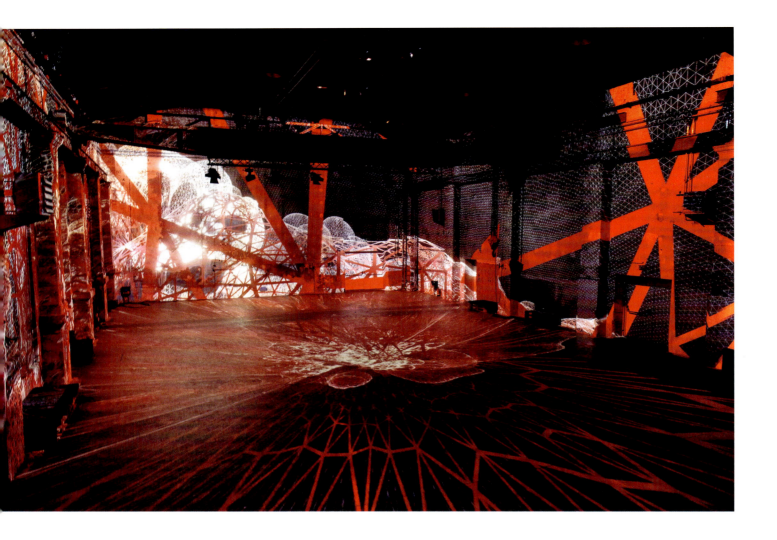

Die cloudbasierte ArtCentrica-Applikation namens TÜBKE TOUCH mit 3000-Gigapixel-Aufnahmen und einer 300 Gigabyte großen Bilddatei erlauben eine Erforschung des Gemäldes bis ins kleinste Detail. Dies ermöglicht die unmittelbare Auseinandersetzung mit dem Kunstwerk, welches im Original allein durch seine gewaltige Größe kaum erfassbar ist. In Zukunft ist ein weltweiter Zugriff auf das Forschungs- und Bildungswerkzeug geplant.

The multimedia installation THE GREAT CIRCLE is a composition by Fischnaller comprising twelve scenes of the panorama painting. In cooperation with Cineca, he developed a script from it and designed dynamic 3D models. These were transmitted in a 27-minute presentation by 25 projectors in a resolution of 21,849 by 2000 pixels onto the 1200-square-metre surface of the machine hall and accompanied by sound effects by Steve Bryson.

The cloud-based ArtCentrica application called TÜBKE TOUCH with 3000 gigapixel shots and a 300 gigabyte image file allow the painting to be researched down to the smallest detail. This enables a direct interaction with the work of art, which can scarcely be grasped in the original due to its mighty size alone. In future, worldwide access to the research and education tool is planned.

Gefördert wird TÜBKE MONUMENTAL von der Ostdeutschen Sparkassenstiftung gemeinsam mit der Sparkasse Leipzig und einer Leipziger Bürgerinitiative.

TÜBKE MONUMENTAL is sponsored by the Ostdeutsche Sparkassenstiftung with Sparkasse Leipzig and a Leipzig civic initiative.

TINY WINDOW CONCERTS
KULTUR KIOSK SARA DAHME, STUTTGART

Location / Client
KULTUR KIOSK, Stuttgart

Month / Year
January – August 2021

Duration
8 months

Awards
*Kulturamt Stuttgart 2021; Sponsorship
"Perspektive Pop" by the MWK BW 2022*

Dramaturgy
Michael Fiedler, Stuttgart (Organisation)

Direction / Coordination
Sara Dahme, Stuttgart

Graphics
Malte Reinisch, Stuttgart

Lighting
Sabrina Schrey, Stuttgart

Films
*Sabrina Schrey, Stuttgart (Camera,
Post-production); Sara Dahme, Stuttgart /
Michael Fiedler, Stuttgart (Camera)*

Music
*Eva Dörr, Stuttgart; Lena Meinhardt,
Stuttgart (Audio recording)*

Artists / Show acts
*Mathias Hartmann; Perigon; KORB;
ANNAGEMINA; HOVING; Nadja Weber;
Malmzeit; Bang & Cherry; JFR Moon;
Vanessa Porter; Marz*

Photos
*Reiner Pfisterer, Ludwigsburg; Sara Dahme,
Stuttgart*

EIN KULTURELLER BEGEGNUNGSORT, DER SICH IN UND MIT DER PANDEMIE ENTWICKELT.

Auch wenn viele Künstler:innen und Kulturschaffende sehr unter der Pandemie gelitten haben, es haben sich dank ihr doch auch neue kulturelle Orte und Formate entwickelt. So wie die Tiny Window Concerts im KULTUR KIOSK. Diese kulturelle Location wurde mitten in der Pandemie, im August 2020, in Stuttgart eröffnet. Die Räumlichkeiten waren zuvor ein Kiosk und Tankstellenladen, heute finden dort Ausstellungen, Konzerte, Lesungen, Workshops und Talks statt. Über die Dauer der Pandemie war der KULTUR KIOSK Gastgeber vieler unterschiedlicher Formate in Präsenz, hybrid und rein digital – es wurde viel experimentiert, um Kunst und Kultur weiterhin sichtbar zu machen und mit anderen ins Gespräch zu kommen.

Even if many artists and those involved in culture suffered greatly under the pandemic, it also sparked the development of new cultural venues and formats, such as the Tiny Window Concerts at the KULTUR KIOSK (culture kiosk). This cultural location was opened in Stuttgart in the midst of the pandemic in August 2020. The premises had previously been a kiosk and petrol station shop, while today exhibitions, concerts, readings, workshops and talks take place there. Throughout the pandemic, many different formats were hosted at the KULTUR KIOSK, whether live, hybrid or purely digital – there was a lot of experimentation in order to continue to make art and culture visible and to enter into dialogue with others.

A PLACE OF CULTURAL ENCOUNTERS, WHICH DEVELOPS WITHIN AND WITH THE PANDEMIC.

Die Tiny Window Concerts entwickelten sich aus einer klassischen Konzertreihe. Die eigentlich mit Publikum geplanten Konzerte konnten zum Teil ins Digitale übertragen werden: Hierzu wurden sie aufgenommen und die fertigen kleinen Videoclips nach und nach auf YouTube veröffentlicht und außen an die Fassade des Kiosks projiziert. Zu Beginn war es Passant:innen nicht erlaubt, am Kiosk stehen zu bleiben; dennoch konnten Fußgängerinnen und Fußgänger im Vorbeischlendern zusehen.

Im Frühjahr 2021 konnten Gäste die Videopremieren wieder vor Ort miterleben. Die Musiker:innen waren entweder direkt vor Ort oder wurden live via Instagram für ein kleines Gespräch dazugeschaltet. So entstand aus einem konventionellen ein hybrides Format, an dem Besuchende über unterschiedliche Schnittstellen teilnehmen können. Die Reihe hat sich zum Publikumsliebling entwickelt und wird 2022 dank einer Förderung des MWK im Rahmen der „Perspektive Pop" weitergeführt.

The Tiny Window Concerts developed from a classical concert series. The concerts, that had actually been planned with spectators, could in part be transferred into a digital format. They were recorded and the finished little video clips were published one by one on YouTube and projected outside on the façade of the kiosk. In the beginning passers-by were not allowed to linger at the kiosk, but pedestrians could watch in passing.

In spring 2021 the guests were able to experience the video premieres live again. The musicians were either directly present on site or were tuned into live via Instagram for a brief discussion. As a result, a conventional became a hybrid format which visitors could participate in through a variety of interfaces. The series developed into a crowd favourite and is being continued in 2022 thanks to funding by MWK as part of the "Perspektive Pop".

ROSINENBAR THF
DIE WELLENMASCHINE GMBH, BERLIN

Location
Tempelhof Airport, Berlin

Client
die wellenmaschine GmbH, Berlin

Month / Year
June – July 2021

Duration
7 weeks (daily)

Dramaturgy
*die wellenmaschine GmbH, Berlin;
Tjabo Reuter, Berlin*

**Direction / Coordination / Architecture /
Design**
die wellenmaschine GmbH, Berlin

Graphics
Michael Welker, Berlin; Tjabo Reuter, Berlin

Lighting
satis&fy AG, Berlin

Music
DJs and bands

Artists / Show acts
*Puerto Hurraco Sisters; Girls Town;
Tangoloft Berlin; Fiedel; Cosmic Noise
and others*

Decoration
*die wellenmaschine GmbH, Berlin;
Rent4Event, Berlin*

Catering
wrap stars, Berlin

Others
*Tempelhof Projekt GmbH, Berlin
(General support)*

Photos
*Gerno Schwidrowski, Berlin; Tjabo Reuter,
Berlin; Uwe Buhrdorf, Berlin*

THE BERLIN CULTURAL SCENE SHOWS ITS DIVERSITY AND DELIGHT AT HOLDING A SHARED EVENT DURING COVID-19.

Im Sommer 2021, nach knapp eineinhalb Jahren Pandemie, war der Wunsch nach Entspannung und gemeinsamen Erlebnissen größer denn je. In dieser Zeit entwickelte die wellenmaschine gemeinsam mit ihrem Partner wrap stars sowie mit der Tempelhof Projekt GmbH als Kooperationspartner ein temporäres Öffnungskonzept für den Flughafen Tempelhof in Berlin. Neben der architektonischen und symbolischen Strahlkraft der Ortes machte man sich auch die Größe im Sinne eines bestmöglichen Infektionsschutzes zunutze.

In the summer of 2021, after around one and a half years of the pandemic, there was a greater yearning for relaxation and shared experiences than ever before. During this time, die wellenmaschine developed a temporary opening concept for the Tempelhof airport in Berlin, together with their partner wrap stars and cooperation partner Tempelhof Projekt GmbH. Apart from the architectural and symbolic charisma of the site, use was also made of its scale in the interests of the best possible infection protection.

The public event under the name of "RosinenBAR THF" was conceived within a few weeks. A "pop-up culture space" was set up on the roofed manoeuvring area, feeling like a mix of an outdoor lounge, open-air cinema and a festival – urban romanticism on the runway, framed and defined by an original raisin bomber.

DIE BERLINER KULTURSZENE ZEIGT IHRE VIELFALT UND FREUDE ÜBER EIN GEMEINSAMES EVENT WÄHREND COVID-19.

Das öffentliche Event unter dem Namen „RosinenBAR THF" wurde innerhalb weniger Wochen konzipiert. Auf dem überdachten Vorfeld entstand ein „pop-up culture space" mit einer Atmosphäre zwischen Outdoor-Lounge, Open-Air-Kino und Festival – urbane Romantik auf dem Rollfeld, umrahmt und bestimmt von einem Original-Rosinenbomber.

Das Programm war bewusst heterogen und griff Literatur, Musik, Film und Tanz auf. Dabei bildete die RosinenBAR THF die Berliner Kultur in großer Breite ab, von Avantgarde bis Mainstream, Berghain-DJs und Jazzbands bis hin zu experimentellen Lesungen. Kinoklassiker griffen sowohl die Stadt Berlin in „Sinfonie einer Großstadt" als auch den Ort selbst in „Nacht über Tempelhof" thematisch auf. Über 4000 Besucher:innen kamen an 60 Tagen – und genossen es, wieder einmal den Flughafen und ein Event live gemeinsam erleben zu können.

KI-KONFERENZ
FACTS AND FICTION GMBH, BERLIN

Location
St. Elisabeth Church, Berlin

Client
Federal Ministry of Labour and
Social Affairs (BMAS) / Policy Lab Digital,
Work and Society, Berlin

Month / Year
May 2021

Duration
2 days

Dramaturgy
Federal Ministry of Labour and Social
Affairs (BMAS), Berlin; 365 Sherpas GmbH,
Berlin; ressourcenmangel GmbH, Berlin;
facts and fiction GmbH, Berlin

Direction / Coordination
Federal Ministry of Labour and Social
Affairs (BMAS), Berlin; facts and fiction
GmbH, Berlin

Architecture / Design / Graphics
facts and fiction GmbH, Berlin

Lighting
JS Medientechnik GmbH & Co. KG, Kassel

Media
365 Sherpas GmbH, Berlin; ressourcenmangel GmbH, Berlin; facts and fiction
GmbH, Berlin

Films
Sympathiefilm GmbH, Berlin

Music
AIVA (aiva.ai)

Catering
Berlin Cuisine Jensen GmbH, Berlin

Photos
J. Konrad Schmidt, Berlin

Die Denkfabrik „Digitale Arbeitsgesellschaft" des BMAS wollte sich mit ihren Aktivitäten und Projekten rund um das Thema KI als Akteurin zeigen und im gegenseitigen Austausch eine Basis für politische Entscheidungen schaffen. Die geplante Konferenz sollte Aspekte der Regulierung und Möglichkeiten einer gemeinwohlorientierten Anwendung von KI-Systemen besprechen sowie Einblicke in die betriebliche Praxis bieten.

EINE HYBRIDE KONFERENZ DISKUTIERT IM ÖFFENTLICHEN AUSTAUSCH DAS THEMA KI.

A HYBRID CONFERENCE PUBLICLY DISCUSSES THE TOPIC OF ARTIFICIAL INTELLIGENCE.

The ministry's Policy Lab Digital, Work and Society wanted to present itself as a campaigner with its activities and projects on the topic of artificial intelligence (AI) and forge a basis for political decisions through mutual exchanges. The planned conference was designed to discuss aspects of the regulation and possibilities of the use of AI systems orientated towards public welfare and to provide insights into operational practice.

Die Agentur facts and fiction entwickelte aufgrund der Pandemie ein digitales bzw. hybrides Konzept, das einen hohen Interaktionsgrad mit den Speakern und dem Publikum enthielt. Um sowohl Fachpublikum als auch die breite Öffentlichkeit zu erreichen, wurde die Veranstaltung als digitales Festival mit verschiedenen inhaltlichen Slots umgesetzt. Zwischen Themenpanels und Sessions gab es in sogenannten WonderMe-Kanälen die Möglichkeit, sich untereinander zu vernetzen oder mit den Redner:innen und Panelist:innen ins Gespräch zu kommen.

Eine Landingpage bündelte alle Streams und Links zu den Sessions sowie Hintergrundinformationen zu den Speakern und Programmpunkten. Auf den Social-Media-Kanälen wurde die Veranstaltung des BMAS und der Denkfabrik unter dem Hashtag #faireki begleitet. Als Studio diente die St.-Elisabeth-Kirche in Berlin-Mitte, die mit ihren unverputzten Wänden einen spannenden Kontrast zu dem eher technisch wahrgenommenen Thema bot. Die Bühnengestaltung war bewusst zurückhaltend gewählt, um die Location durch eine akzentuierte Beleuchtung auch im Stream zur Geltung kommen zu lassen.

Due to the pandemic, the agency facts and fiction developed a digital and hybrid concept for this that comprised a high degree of interaction with the speakers and the public. In order to reach both specialists and the wider public, the event was realised as digital festival with a variety of content slots. In between themed panels and sessions, the so-called WonderMe channels provided the opportunity for networking or discussing with the speakers and panelists.

A landing page brought together all the streams and links to the sessions, as well as background information about the speakers and programme items. The BMAS and think tank event was accompanied on social media channels under the hashtag #faireki. The St. Elisabeth Church in Berlin-Mitte served as a studio, its unplastered walls forming an interesting contrast to the topic that appeared rather technical. The stage design was deliberately modest in order to highlight the venue also in the stream by means of accentuated lighting.

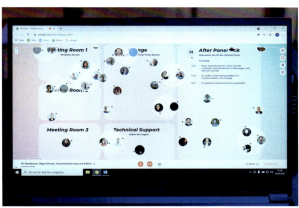

UNZEEN GAMING STUDIO CONCEPT
MIKS GMBH BRAND SPACE DESIGN, HAMBURG

Location
Hamburg, others

Client
*unzeen Investorengemeinschaft
Jakob Braendle, Hamburg*

Month / Year
Spring 2020 (Beginning)

Duration
Several months

Awards
*Gold at BrandEx 2022 (Best Cancelled
Project)*

**Dramaturgy / Direction / Coordination /
Architecture / Design / Graphics**
MIKS brand space design, Hamburg

Construction
*Kaether & Weise GmbH Möbelbau,
Lamspringe*

Photos
MIKS brand space design, Hamburg

EIN VR-GAMING-STUDIO-KONZEPT, DAS GEMEINSAME SPIELERLEBNISSE UND SPORTLICHE WETTKÄMPFE VERBINDET.

A group of investors from the areas of real estate, IT, incentives and sports/events venues planned to build up a chain of VR gaming studios. The aim was to introduce a concept to the German market that appealed to the majority of urban consumers, encouraging regular visits. The games were to be a mix of different styles, amongst others such resembling the comic-like Moorhuhn series, fairytale fantasy worlds with big nature scenes, or war games with sinister settings. MIKS developed a digital and spatial corporate identity concept for this, with a design focus on the meta theme of "game".

Eine Gruppe von Investoren aus den Bereichen Immobilien, IT, Incentive und Sport-/Eventstätten hatte den Plan, eine Kette von VR-Gaming-Studios aufzubauen. Der deutsche Markt sollte mit einem Konzept besetzt werden, das den Großteil der urbanen Konsument:innen anspricht und sie zu regelmäßigen Besuchen anregt. Die Spiele sollten eine Mischung sein, unter anderem aus Games im Comicstil von Moorhuhn, märchenhaften Fantasywelten mit großen Naturszenen oder Wargames mit düsteren Umgebungen. MIKS entwickelte hierfür ein digitales und räumliches Corporate-Identity-Konzept, welches das Meta-Thema „Spiel" gestalterisch in den Mittelpunkt stellt.

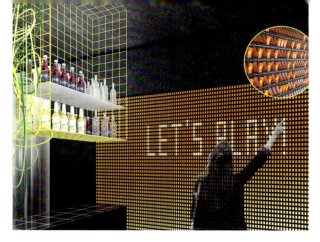

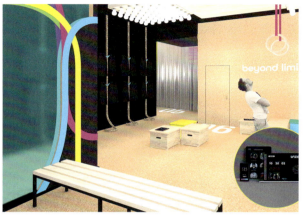

A VR GAMING STUDIO CONCEPT THAT COMBINES SHARED GAMING EXPERIENCES AND SPORTS COMPETITIONS.

Ziel und Botschaft sind der Fokus auf das Erlebnis und die Gemeinsamkeit. Ein Erlebnis mit Freundinnen, Freunden, mit der ganzen Familie oder den Gaming-Stars vor Ort. Ein Ort, der Austausch, sportlichen Wettkampf und gemeinsame Begeisterung ermöglicht. Dabei findet sich die Verbindung von analogen und virtuellen Welten auch in der medialen Verkreuzung wieder: Onlineportal und Onsite-Erlebnis, App und die Option, mit eigener Ausstattung zu Hause zu spielen.

Logo und CI sind von den Licht- und Nichtfarben RGB, Schwarz und Weiß geprägt. Der Raum bedient Gegensätze und Brüche: Analog und Digital, Gestern und Morgen, Holz und Metall. Semitransparente Vorhänge mit metallischen Effekten gehen auf das unterschiedliche Bedürfnis nach Privatsphäre beim Gaming ein. Auf Science-Fiction-Klischees wie etwa Star-Wars-Schwebetüren wurde bewusst verzichtet, um das Erlebnis ganz im Heute zu platzieren.

The aim and message are a focus on experiences and togetherness. An experience with friends, with the whole family or the gaming stars on site. A place that enables interaction, sports competitions and shared enthusiasm. The combination of analogue and virtual worlds is also reflected in the media mix: online portal and on-site experience, an app and the option of playing with one's own equipment at home.

The logo and corporate identity are characterised by the light colours and non-colours of RGB, black and white. The space displays contrasts and tangents: analogue and digital, yesterday and tomorrow, wood and metal. Semi-transparent curtains with metallic effects meet different requirements for privacy while gaming. Science fiction clichés such as Star Wars floating doors were deliberately avoided to position the experience fully in the here and now.

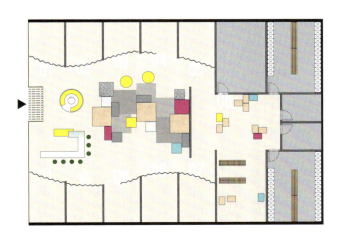

MITTENDRIN
SCENEDELUXE – ANDREA BOHACZ, LÜBECK

Location
Urban space, Lübeck

Client
KulturFunke Lübeck*

Month / Year
August 2021

Duration
Several days

Direction / Coordination
SceneDeluxe – Andrea Bohacz, Lübeck

Media
Christoffer Greiß Seitenumsatz, Lübeck

Artists / Show acts
Several authors and speakers

Photos
Christoffer Greiß Seitenumsatz, Lübeck

Im zweiten Corona-Frühjahr 2021 kam die Künstlergruppe SceneDeluxe auf die Frage: Was wäre, wenn zur Wahrung des Abstands die dritte Dimension – die Höhe – einbezogen würde? Ihre Antwort darauf: eine unkonventionelle öffentliche Installation namens „MITTENDRIN – Ein Stuhl im Irgendwo".

Für MITTENDRIN positionierten sie einen hohen Stuhl auf einem alltäglichen belebten Platz in Lübeck. Oben, auf 1,83 Metern Sitzhöhe, befand sich ein Noise-Cancelling-Kopfhörer mit einer Tonbox. Wer sich traute, kletterte hoch und nahm Platz, um ein ganz besonderes Hör- und Seherlebnis zu genießen.

A PUBLIC ART AND AUDIO EXPERIENCE AT A HEIGHT OF AROUND TWO METRES IN COMPLIANCE WITH CORONA-VIRUS DISTANCING.

In the second corona spring 2021, the question arose for the artist group SceneDeluxe: What if the third dimension – height – were taken into consideration for maintaining distance? Their answer to this was an unconventional public installation called "MITTENDRIN – Ein Stuhl im Irgendwo" ('IN THE MIDST – A Chair Somewhere'),

For MITTENDRIN, they positioned a high chair on a popular square in Lübeck. Up at a sitting height of 1.83 metres there were noise-cancelling headphones with a sound box. Whoever dared could climb up and take a seat to enjoy a very special audiovisual experience.

EIN ÖFFENTLICHES KUNST- UND HÖRERLEBNIS MIT COVID-KONFORMEM ABSTAND IN KNAPP ZWEI METERN HÖHE.

Für die Aktion, die erstmals im August 2021 an vier verschiedenen Orten in Lübeck stattfand, schrieben Lübecker Autor:innen jeweils exklusive, kurze Kolumnen. Dabei nahmen die Hörstücke inhaltlich Bezug auf den jeweiligen Ort, wo der Hörhochstuhl aufgestellt wurde – und damit auch auf die „Aussicht" der Hörenden. So teilte der Schauspieler Peter Grünig am Travemünder Hundestrand mit der Geschichte „Einer hatte eine Gitarre dabei" Jugenderinnerungen des Kolumnisten Maximilian Buddenbohm; Künstlerin Nicola Reinitzer las „Krähenfüße und Krähenflügel" von HannaH Rau, die gewinnend Parallelen zu einer Showtreppe ins Altstadtbad Krähenteich zog; und im Baumarkt legte Sigrid Dettlof (Theater Combinale) den komplexen und langwierigen Entscheidungsprozess für oder gegen die Anschaffung einer 10-Meter-Alu-Ausziehleiter kompromisslos offen („Wohlfühlzone Baumarkt", Autorin: Majka Gerke).

Eine ungewöhnliche Plattform für die Lübecker Autor:innen, Vorleser:innen und zuhörenden Menschen, die 2022 eine Fortsetzung findet. Ein gutes Stück über der Alltagssituation und im gleichen Moment eben „mittendrin".

Lübeck authors wrote exclusive short columns for the event, which took place for the first time in August 2021 at four different locations in Lübeck. The content of the audio pieces referred to the respective location where the audio highchair was set up – and therefore also to the "view" for the listeners. For example, at the Travemünde dog beach the actor peter Grünig recounted youth memories of the columnist Maximilian Buddenbohm with the story "Einer hatte eine Gitarre dabei" ('One had a Guitar with him'), the artist Nicola Reinitzer read "Krähenfüße und Krähenflügel" ('Crow's Feet and Crow's Wings') by HannaH Rau and at the DIY market Sigrid Dettlof (Theater Combinale) uncompromisingly revealed the complex and arduous decision-making process for or against the acquisition of a 10-metre extendable aluminium ladder ("Wohlfühlzone Baumarkt" / 'Building Market Wellness Zone', author: Majka Gerke).

It was an unusual platform for the Lübeck authors, readers and listeners, to be continued in 2022. High above everyday life and at the same time "in the midst" of things.

2021 EQS CHINA ROAD SHOW
UNIPLAN GMBH & CO. KG, COLOGNE

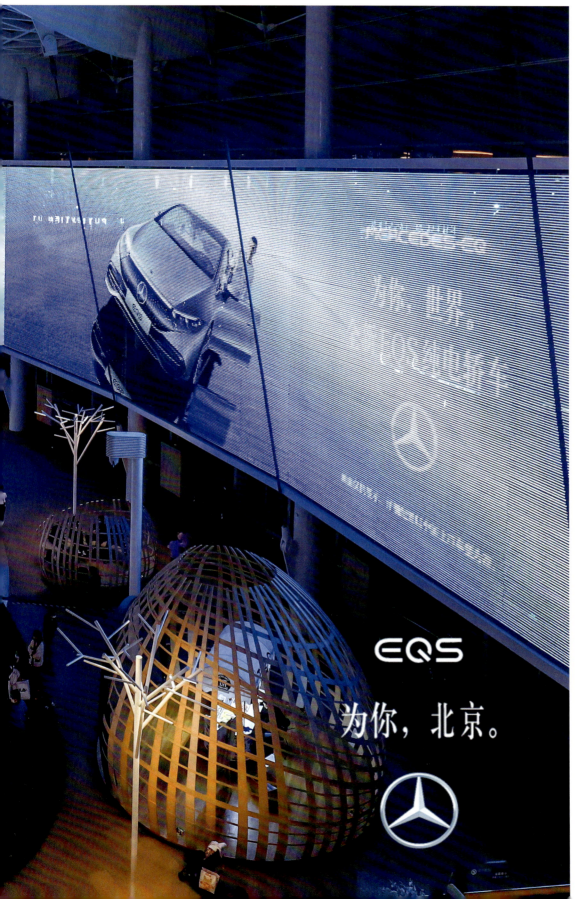

Locations
10 Chinese cities: Beijing, Suzhou, Hangzhou, Shanghai, Shenzhen, Haikou, Zhengzhou, Xian, Chengdu, Changsha

Client
Mercedes-EQ, Stuttgart

Month / Year
May – July 2021

Duration
2 1/2 months

Awards
Silver at Global Eventex Awards 2022 (Brand Experience – Automotive)

Architecture / Design
Atelier I-N-D-J, Shanghai

Lighting
Kingsmark Limited, Beijing

Media
Kingsmark Limited, Beijing (Audio-visuals); GMUNK Inc. Tool of North America, Berkeley (Multimedia art)

Construction
UTRUST, Shanghai

Photos
Wang Xin, Beijing; Zhan Hui, Beijing

EIN MOBILER RAUM MIT FUTURISTI-SCHEN ERLEBNISSEN PRÄSENTIERT EIN E-AUTO UND SEINE MARKE.

Der neue EQS von Mercedes-EQ ist das erste vollelektrische Luxusfahrzeug des Autobauers. Um den EQS der Öffentlichkeit vorzustellen und die Wahrnehmung der Marke Mercedes-EQ in China zu stärken, entwickelte Uniplan eine Roadshow, die trotz pandemischer Herausforderungen in zehn chinesischen Städten Station machte.

The new EQS by Mercedes-EQ is the car manufacturer's first fully electric luxury vehicle. To present EQS to the public and to strengthen the presence of the Mercedes-EQ brand in China, Uniplan developed a roadshow that halted in ten Chinese cities despite the challenges of the pandemic.

A MOBILE SPACE WITH FUTURISTIC EXPERIENCES PRESENTS AN ELECTRIC CAR AND ITS BRAND.

In Zusammenarbeit mit Künstlern und Kooperationspartnern wurde ein Raum voll futuristischer Technologieerlebnisse gestaltet. Er sollte Nachhaltigkeit und Technologie verbinden und zu neuen Ideen für eine bessere Zukunft inspirieren.

In cooperation with artists and partners, a space full of futuristic technology experiences was created. It was designed to combine sustainability and technology and to inspire new ideas for a better future.

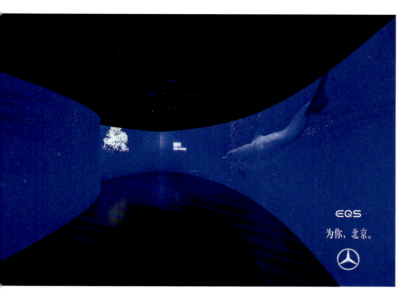

Der mit dem Designstudio Atelier I-N-D-J entworfene Pavillon sorgte bereits mit der Fassade, die Medienarchitektur und optische Täuschungen miteinander kombinierte, für Aufsehen. Im Inneren erwarteten die Besuchenden verschiedene Inhalte und Filme. Darunter eine Geschichte, die das Publikum in die Zukunft mitnahm und dazu einlud, sich die Welt von morgen vorzustellen. Ein weiteres Highlight war der abstrakte Film des Multimedia-Künstlers GMUNK, der ein immersives und sinnliches Erlebnis erzeugen sollte.

The pavilion designed with the studio Atelier I-N-D-J caused a stir with its façade alone, which combined the media architecture and optical illusions. In the interior, a variety of content and films awaited the visitors. It included a story that transported the public into the future and invited them to imagine the world of tomorrow. A further highlight was the abstract film by multimedia artist GMUNK, which aimed at generating an immersive and sensory experience.

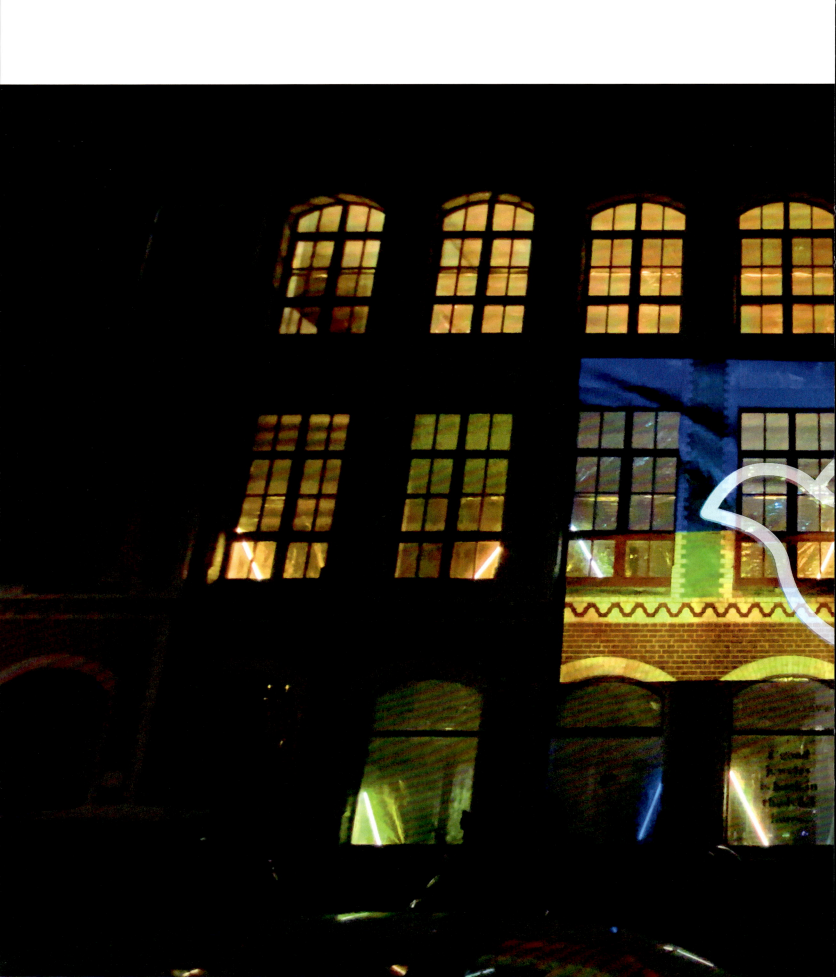

PUBLIC

JASMINA JOVY JEWELRY SHOWROOM PREVENT
STEFFEN VETTERLE, STUTTGART;
JASMINA JOVY JEWELRY, PFORZHEIM / STUTTGART

Location
Showroom and studio, Pforzheim

Client
Jasmina Jovy Jewelry, Pforzheim / Stuttgart

Month / Year
March 2022

Duration
1 day (Event), 2 months (Installation)

Dramaturgy / Films
Steffen Vetterle, Stuttgart

Direction / Coordination / Architecture / Design
Steffen Vetterle, Stuttgart; Jasmina Jovy, Pforzheim

Graphics
Jasmina Jovy, Pforzheim

Lighting
Konrad Prosser; Georg Wienert; Marius Holzinger; Severin Schröder; Marko Kubitza; Steffen Vetterle

Media
Steffen Vetterle (Façade and interior projection)

Music / Artists / Show acts
Stella Muriel Müller

Decoration
Monika Markert; Konrad Prosser; Georg Wienert; Marius Holzinger; Katharina Dombrowsky; Anastasiya Yavorska; Christina Buchner; Katharina Daunhawer; Grit Kunze; Stella Muriel Müller; Tony Montana; Steffen Vetterle; Jasmina Jovy

Catering
Café / Bar Rodensteiner, Pforzheim; Applaus Stuttgart Dry Gin Dulay-Winkler, Büttner, Frey GbR, Stuttgart, Elephant Bay GmbH, Stuttgart (Drink sponsoring)

Photos
Marius Holzinger, Stuttgart; Steffen Vetterle, Stuttgart

EINE SCHLICHTE, MEHRDEUTIGE UND EFFEKTVOLLE FASSADEN-INSTALLATION ALS PR- UND SPENDENAKTION.

In order to announce the opening of a showroom for the jewellery designer Jasmina Jovy at the Pforzheim office building "Kollmar & Jourdan", as well as to revitalise a district and at the same time collect money for a charitable purpose, a multifaceted and effective façade installation was created. In accordance with a directorial idea by Steffen Vetterle, the windows of the iconic office building were veiled with gold foil with the help of volunteers. By the time of the opening on 5/14/2022, the façade was given a distinctive golden sheen over three floors.

"Gold" and its brilliance were critically questioned in the self-proclaimed gold town of Pforzheim: The gold foil, which turns out to be a conventional rescue blanket, does not only represent obvious glamour and luxury in the artistic concept. A rescue blanket normally serves the purpose of protecting people in an emergency. It evokes all refugees – on this evening and in the current context of Ukraine.

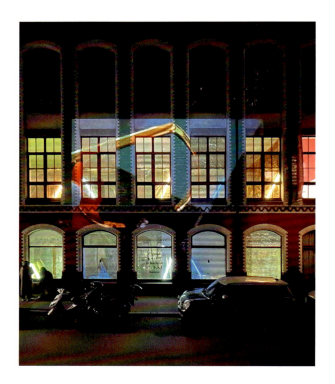

Um die Eröffnung eines Showrooms der Schmuckdesignerin Jasmina Jovy im Pforzheimer Kontorgebäude „Kollmar & Jourdan" anzukündigen, ein Stadtviertel wiederzubeleben und zugleich Geld für einen karitativen Zweck zu sammeln, entstand eine mehrdeutige und effektvolle Fassadeninstallation. Nach einer inszenatorischen Idee von Steffen Vetterle wurden mithilfe von Freiwilligen die Fenster des ikonischen Kontorgebäudes in Goldfolie gehüllt. Über drei Geschosse hinweg bis zur Eröffnung am 14.05.2022 erhielt die Fassade einen prägnanten güldenen Glanz.

Dabei wurde „Gold" und dessen Glanz in der selbsternannten Goldstadt Pforzheim kritisch hinterfragt: Die Goldfolie, die sich als normale Rettungsdecke entpuppt, bedeutet im künstlerischen Konzept nicht nur den offensichtlichen Glamour und Luxus. Die Rettungsdecke dient normalerweise dazu, Notleidende zu schützen. Sie erinnert sinnbildlich an alle Flüchtenden – an diesem Abend und im gegenwärtigen Kontext der Ukraine.

Die öffentlichkeitswirksame Pro-bono-Aktion aller Beteiligten samt Ausstellung und Abendevent sollte nach der Coronazeit verschiedenste Menschen zusammenbringen, Spendengelder sammeln – und nicht zuletzt das Stadtviertel beleben sowie als den neuen kreativen Hub kommunizieren.

Die Goldfolien der Installation wurden später durch die Pforzheimer Modedesignerin Monika Markert in Taschen umgearbeitet. Diese fanden bei der Showroom-Eröffnung als Goodiebags Verwendung und können käuflich erworben werden.

A SIMPLE, MULTIFACETED AND EFFECTIVE FAÇADE INSTALLATION AS A PR AND FUND-RAISING CAMPAIGN.

The publicly effective pro bono campaign by all those involved, together with the exhibition and evening event, was designed to bring a variety of people together after the coronavirus period, to gather donations and not least to revitalise the district and communicate it as a new creative hub.

The gold foil of the installation was being converted into bags later by the Pforzheim fashion designer Monika Markert. These were being used in the showroom opening as goodie bags and are available for purchase.

CULTURE LAB @CAMPUS GERMANY
VOSS+FISCHER GMBH, FRANKFURT AM MAIN;
MIKE P. HEISEL, MUNICH

Location
German Pavilion at the Expo 2020 Dubai

Client
Federal Ministry for Economic Affairs and
Climate Action, Berlin

Month / Year
October 2021 – March 2022

Duration
27 weeks

Dramaturgy / Direction / Coordination
VOSS+FISCHER GmbH, Frankfurt am
Main; Mike P. Heisel, Munich

Graphics
Roman Lorenz, Hanover

Lighting
sld mediatec, Nuremberg

Artists / Show Acts
Music Session: Wolf & Moon; Beatelephant;
Myle; Listen to Jules; Roast Apple; RIIVA;
Mad Hatter's Daughter; In Between; Boundz;
June Cocó; Konstantin Reinfeld; No Chance;
HfM Weimar; JILX; Musikkorps der Bundes-
wehr, Sextett; Lienne; Ameli Paul / Dance
Session: ADTV; Just in Time; Step Up Acade-
my; Berlicious / Art Session: Vrady

Others
Henkel Forschwerwelt, Dusseldorf;
Miele & Cie. KG, Gütersloh (Cooperation for
various event concepts)

Photos
Sofiya Kartasheva, Dubai; Bjoern Lauen,
Dubai; Dario Suppan, Munich

Der Deutsche Pavillon auf der Expo 2020 Dubai präsentierte sich als Ort der Innovation und Forschung, als CAMPUS GERMANY. An seine drei Labore – das Energy Lab, das Future City Lab und das Biodiversity Lab – knüpfte auch das von VOSS+FISCHER betreute und von Mike P. Heisel kuratierte Culture Lab an: ein partizipatives Kulturprogramm, dessen Spektrum die kulturelle Vielfalt Deutschlands präsentierte. Angelehnt an das Thema der Expo „Connecting Minds, Creating the Future" verstand es sich als Plattform interkultureller Begegnung.

A PARTICIPATORY CULTURE PROGRAMME CONVEYS THE GERMAN CULTURAL AND CREATIVE LANDSCAPE.

EIN PARTIZIPATIVES KULTURPROGRAMM VERMITTELT DIE DEUTSCHE KULTUR- UND KREATIV- LANDSCHAFT.

The German pavilion at Expo 2020 Dubai presented itself as a hub of innovation and research, as CAMPUS GERMANY. The Culture Lab handled by VOSS+FISCHER and curated by Mike P. Hensel – a participatory culture programme whose spectrum presented the cultural diversity of Germany – was also based on its three laboratories: the Energy Lab, the Future City Lab and the Biodiversity Lab. In line with the theme of the Expo "Connecting Minds, Creating the Future", it represented a platform for intercultural encounters.

Zusammengesetzt aus sechs „Sessions" verband das Culture Lab Musik, Tanz, visuelle Künste, Gaming, Sport und Wissenschaft. Neben Nachwuchstalenten setzten international bekannte Künstler:innen, Persönlichkeiten und Acts Highlights.

Die Music Sessions brachten die deutsche Musikszene sowie ein mehrwöchiges Musicalprogramm auf die Bühne. Bei den Dance Sessions luden Formationen wie „Together We Move" zum Mittanzen ein. Zudem überraschten die Tanzlehrer des ADTV und das Pavillonteam die Gäste gelegentlich mit einer eigens konzipierten Choreografie zum CAMPUS GERMANY. Kunstprojekte und Installationen in Verbindung mit neuen Technologien griffen das Thema „Connecting Minds, Creating the Future" auf und gaben Einblicke in die Werke von Nachwuchskünstler:innen.

Bei den Games Sessions konnten Besuchende jedes Alters aktuellste Entwicklungen entdecken und ausprobieren. Einmal wöchentlich fand der eSports Day statt, der zum Mitspielen an den Konsolen animierte. Bei den Sport Sessions wurden Live-Übertragungen deutscher Sportevents geboten und durch Quizzes den Besuchern die deutsche Sportkultur näher gebracht. Es gab Sportangebote für Kinder und Jugendliche bis hin zu Urban Street Performances. Die Science Sessions stellten in Vorträgen, Filmen oder Mitmach-Experimenten deutsche Technologien und Innovationen vor. Hier wurde geforscht, gelernt, getüftelt und entdeckt.

Comprising six "sessions", the Culture Lab brought together music, dance, visual arts, gaming, sport and science. Apart from up-and-coming talents, highlights included internationally known artists, personalities and acts.

The music sessions brought the German music scene and a multi-week musical programme onto the stage. During the dance sessions, formations such as "Together We Move" invited participants to join in the dancing. The Pavilion team and the ADTV's dance instructors also occasionally surprised the guests with a choreography conceived exclusively for CAMPUS GERMANY. Art projects and installations in combination with new technologies took up the theme of "Connecting Minds, Creating the Future" and provided insights into the works of up-and-coming artists.

During the games sessions, visitors of all ages were able to discover and try out the latest developments. The eSports day took place once a week, encouraging playing at the consoles. As part of the sports sessions, live transmissions of German sports events were offered and visitors could learn about German sports culture in quizzes. There were sports offers for children and young people, as well as urban street performances. Technologies and innovations from Germany were introduced during the science sessions by means of presentations, films or participatory experiments, allowing research, learning, trying out and discovering.

Jede Zielgruppe hat unterschiedliche Bedürfnisse und Erwartungen. Dementsprechend sind Eventkonzepte im Idealfall nicht nur auf den Absender, sondern vor allem auf die Empfänger zugeschnitten.

PARTNERS: VERBUNDENE UNTERNEHMEN, (ZWISCHEN-) HÄNDLER ODER VERTRIEBS- PARTNER, DEREN INFORMA- TIONSHINTERGRUND BEREITS AUF EINE EBENE GEBRACHT WURDE ODER NUN GEBRACHT WERDEN SOLL. DEMENT- SPRECHEND HOMOGEN IST DIESE ZIELGRUPPE ZUSAMMEN- GESTELLT, DEREN ANSPRACHE DIREKT UND EXTREM ZIEL- ORIENTIERT GEHANDHABT WERDEN KANN.

Each target group has different requirements and expectations. Event concepts are therefore ideally not only geared towards the addressor, but especially towards the recipients.

PARTNERS: THESE ARE ASSOCIATED COMPANIES, (INTERMEDIARY) DISTRIBUTORS OR SALES PARTNERS WHO ALREADY HAVE A CERTAIN LEVEL OF BACKGROUND INFORMATION, OR FOR WHOM THIS IS NOW TO BE PROVIDED. THIS TARGET GROUP THEREFORE HAS A HOMOGENEOUS COMPOSITION AND CAN BE APPEALED TO DIRECTLY AND IN A VERY TARGET-ORIENTATED MANNER.

VODAFONE KICK-OFFS 2021
INSGLÜCK GESELLSCHAFT FÜR MARKEN-INSZENIERUNG MBH, BERLIN

Location
Lichtburg Essen

Client
Vodafone GmbH, Dusseldorf

Month / Year
May 2021

Duration
3 days

Dramaturgy
insglück Christoph Kirst / Frederik Nimmesgern, Berlin & Cologne

Direction / Coordination
insglück Jörg Wickert / Florian Schneiderhan, Cologne (Overall direction); Jan Niclas Schatka, Bergheim (Programme direction)

Architecture / Design
insglück David Tschechne, Hamburg; Katrin Hampus, Munich

Graphics
insglück Janina Quante, Cologne

Lighting
Loud GmbH, Breuna

Media
insglück Alexander Rose, Berlin; Elberfeld Kreation, Wuppertal

Films
insglück Daniel Frerix, Cologne; Elberfeld Kreation, Wuppertal

Music
Extreme music, Berlin

Artists / Show acts
music4friends entertainment gmbh, Wuppertal; René Travnicek, Dusseldorf

Decoration
BALLONI GmbH, Cologne

Catering
DEINspeisesalon, Cologne

Construction
Loud GmbH, Breuna; BALLONI GmbH, Cologne

Others
Loud GmbH, Breuna (Technology); tough solutions GmbH, Breuna (Digital streaming platform)

Photos
Markus Arns FacesAndMore, Herten

EIN AKTIVIERENDES DIGITALFORMAT VERNETZT RUND 5000 VODAFONE-VERTRIEBLER:INNEN.

The aim was to activate and network around 5000 German Vodafone sales employees under the motto of "The Spirit of Giga". The focus of the three-day, dynamic, digital kick-off was on information, motivation and appreciation. The handling agency insglück chose Lichtburg Essen for the live broadcast, Germany's largest film palace, providing an atmospheric and festive setting for the event.

Unter dem Motto „The Spirit of Giga" sollten rund 5000 deutsche Vodafone-Mitarbeiter:innen aus dem Vertrieb aktiviert und untereinander vernetzt werden. Im Fokus des dreitägigen, dynamischen digitalen Kick-offs standen Information, Motivation und Wertschätzung. Für die Live-Übertragung wählte die betreuende Agentur insglück die Lichtburg Essen, Deutschlands größten Filmpalast, der somit eine atmosphärische und festlich anmutende Kulisse für das Geschehen bot.

AN ACTIVATING DIGITAL FORMAT NETWORKS AROUND 5000 VODAFONE SALESPEOPLE.

An individualised event platform allowed the employees to take part in the show through a total of eight two-hour streams. The action could be controlled by means of so-called spirit buttons, enabling a variety of interaction.

The integrated applause and emoji functions were translated into acoustic and visual signals and transmitted to the hall, which had rows of two-dimensional employee figures as spectators.

Über eine individualisierte Eventplattform war es den Mitarbeitenden möglich, an insgesamt acht je zweistündigen Streams an der Show teilzunehmen. Mittels sogenannter Spirit-Buttons konnte dabei das Geschehen gesteuert und auf verschiedene Art interagiert werden.

Die integrierten Applaus- und Emoji-Funktionen wurden in akustische und visuelle Signale übersetzt und in den von zweidimensionalen Mitarbeiter-Figuren in den Publikumsrängen bevölkerten Saal übertragen.

HENDRICK'S GRAND HOTEL
PROOF & SONS GMBH & CO. KG, BERLIN; ZWANZIGZWANZIG GMBH, BERLIN

Location
The Grand, Berlin

Client
William Grant & Sons Brands Ltd, Bellshill

Month / Year
August 2021

Duration
5 days

Graphics
S. Milenovic, Hamburg

Artists / Show acts
The Gazebo Effect, London

Decoration
BALLONI GmbH, Berlin

Catering
Taube Grau, Berlin; Barthur Barcatering GmbH, Berlin; PARS Pralinen, Berlin

Photos
Steven Kohl, Zurich; Hauke Thüring, Berlin

EINE KURIOSE UND SPIELERISCHE REISE IN DAS INSZENIERTE „GRAND HOTEL" EINER GINMARKE.

Nachdem das Reisen über zwei Jahre hinweg nur begrenzt möglich war, wollte Hendrick's Gin seine Gäste im August 2021 mit einem „Urlaubserlebnis" beschenken. Im Auftrag der Kreativagentur Proof & Sons inszenierte die Agentur zwanzigzwanzig das „Hendrick's Grand Hotel" – eine fünf-tägige, coronakonforme Brand-Aktivierung.

After travelling had only been possible to a limited extent over a period of two years, Hendrick's gin wanted to gift its guests a "holiday experience" in August 2021. On behalf of the creative agency Proof & Sons, the agency zwanzig-zwanzig staged the "Hendrick's Grand Hotel" – a five-day brand campaign in line with corona regulations.

For this, they transformed the fine dining restaurant "The Grand Berlin" into the Hendrick's Grand Hotel – an immersive and highly curious brand experience. On the search for "their" room, the 37 small groups were accompanied by actors and actresses who slipped into the roles of hotel staff. For the decoration and setting the scene, 600 roses and 1125 cucumbers were used – both central components of Hendrick's Gin.

A CURIOUS AND PLAYFUL JOURNEY INTO THE STAGED "GRAND HOTEL" OF A GIN BRAND.

The journey of the "travel groups" started at the reception: The British hotel personnel in the form of a bellboy, a caretaker, the hotel director, a cucumbologist and a cleansing master took the guests with them on a tour through the hotel, in which they were always part of the staging. During the tour, gin drinks and cucumber snacks were served, whilst the history of Hendrick's Gin surrounding the Scottish master distiller Lesley Gracie was told playfully. The highlights of the tour included a tongue-in-cheek "cucumber cleansing ritual" at the beginning, in order to cast off the noise of the city and settle into the hotel. Among further highlights were a suitcase auction in the "Lost & Found Room", a gin teatime with cucumber macarons and rose shortbread, as well as a spontaneous "CURIOSITY" quiz in the staff lift. On their tour, the guests collected goodies along the way for their Hendrick's Gin toiletry bag.

Hierfür verwandelten sie das Fine-Dining-Restaurant „The Grand Berlin" in das Hendrick's Grand Hotel – eine immersive und höchst kuriose Marken-Experience. Auf der vermeintlichen Suche nach „ihrem" gebuchten Hotelzimmer wurden die insgesamt 37 Kleingruppen durch Schauspieler:innen begleitet, die in die Rolle des Hotelpersonals schlüpften. Für die Dekoration und Inszenierung wurden knapp 600 Rosen und 1125 Gurken verwendet – beides zentrale Bestandteile von Hendrick's Gin.

Die Journey der „Reisegruppen" startete an der Rezeption: Das britische Hotelpersonal in Form eines Bellboys, eines Hausmeisters, des Hoteldirektors, einer Cucumbologist und einem Cleansing Master nahmen die Gäste mit auf eine Tour durch das Hotel, in der sie stets Teil der Inszenierung waren. Während des Rundgangs wurden Gin-Drinks und Gurkensnacks serviert und dabei spielerisch die Geschichte von Hendrick's Gin rund um die schottische Meister-Destillateurin Lesley Gracie erzählt. Zu den Highlights der Tour gehörten ein mit Augenzwinkern zu verstehendes „Cucumber Cleansing Ritual" zu Beginn, um den Lärm der Stadt abzulegen und sich für das Hotel zu öffnen. Weitere Highlights waren eine Kofferauktion im „Lost & Found Room", eine Gin-Teatime mit Gurkenmacarons und Rosen-Shortbread sowie ein spontanes „CURIOSITY"-Quiz im Hotel-Aufzug. Während der Tour sammelten die Gäste auf ihrem Weg Goodies für ihren Hendrick's Gin-Kulturbeutel.

EBAY OPEN 2020.DIGITAL
INSGLÜCK GESELLSCHAFT FÜR MARKEN-INSZENIERUNG MBH, BERLIN

Location
eBay Campus, Dreilinden

Client
eBay GmbH, Kleinmachnow

Month / Year
October 2020

Duration
Several days (20 hours live, 20 days
on demand)

Awards
2 × Silver (Best Corporate, Best Conference)
at BrandEx 2022; Gold (Corporate/b2b)
and Silver (Community Involvement) at
Galaxy Awards 2021

Dramaturgy
insglück Frederik Nimmesgern /
Tobias Bergmann, Cologne

Direction / Coordination
insglück Amelie Müller / Heike Rose, Berlin
(Overall direction); Christian Legler, Berlin;
Harry Seedorf, Berlin; Martha Gerber-
Wagner, Berlin

Graphics
insglück Dilara Keskinler / Janina Quante /
Uta Krüger, Cologne & Berlin

Media
insglück Alexander Rose / David Tschechne,
Berlin & Hamburg

Music
Billy Burrito

Artists / Show acts
eBay Crew; Yasmine Blair (Moderator)

Construction
Neumann & Müller GmbH & Co. KG,
Taufkirchen; WE Make it GmbH, Königs
Wusterhausen

Others
doo GmbH, Munich; FAKTOR 3 AG,
Hamburg; FastLane GmbH, Bonn; pioneer
communications Holding GmbH, Leipzig;
teambits GmbH, Darmstadt; voodoopop
studios, Berlin

Photos
Patricia Kalisch, Berlin

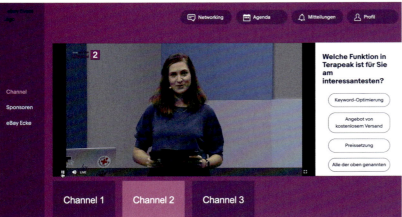

2019 trafen sich bei der eBay Open über 800 gewerbliche Verkäufer:innen in Berlin, um sich mit der Community und eBay-Expert:innen auszutauschen. 2020 war das pandemiebedingt nicht möglich. So entstand in Zusammenarbeit mit insglück eine digitale Alternative: die eBay Open 2020.digital. Das Ziel: ein Event implementieren, das Informationen vermittelt, Vertrauen schafft, die Gemeinschaft der Verkäufer:innen stärkt und ihre Loyalität zur Marke festigt. In diesem Sinne öffnete eBay seine Türen und gab der deutschen Verkäufer:innen-Community einen direkten Einblick. Während der zweitägigen Veranstaltung verwandelte sich der eBay-Campus in Dreilinden in ein Sendezentrum.

A DIGITAL EVENT. THREE CHANNELS. A 20-HOUR PROGRAMME WITH EXCLUSIVE CONTENT AND DISCUSSIONS.

Over 800 sellers met at the eBay Open in 2019 in Berlin to mingle with the community and eBay experts. It was not possible in 2020 due to the pandemic. This led to a digital alternative in cooperation with insglück: the eBay Open 2020.digital. The aim was to realise an event that conveys information, inspires trust, strengthens the sales community and consolidates their loyalty to the brand. It was in this spirit that eBay opened its doors, giving the German seller community a direct insight. During the two-day event, the eBay campus in Dreilinden was transformed into a broadcasting centre.

Die Verkäufer:innen erhielten 20 Stunden eBay-Know-how sowie 20 Tage lang exklusive Inhalte on demand. Fast 60 eBayer waren an der Produktion und Organisation hinter den Kulissen beteiligt. Manager und Teammitglieder schlüpften vor der Kamera in verschiedene Rollen. Es entstand ein informatives und maßgeschneidertes Programm: Nachrichtensendungen, Talkshows, Dokumentationen und Berichte hinter den Kulissen. Prominente Expert:innen teilten ihr eBay-Knowhow in Vorträgen und Diskussionsrunden.

EIN DIGITALES EVENT. DREI KANÄLE. 20 STUNDEN PROGRAMM MIT EXKLUSIVEN INHALTEN UND AUSTAUSCH.

Den Teilnehmenden wurde ein eigener Kanal zur Verfügung gestellt, um Best Practices und interaktive Sessions anzubieten. Sie konnten sich mit Gästen austauschen, an Diskussionen teilnehmen und ihre Meinungen in Umfragen bekannt geben. Den Abschluss bildete eine unterhaltsame Late Night Show mit Quiz, Band, der Verleihung der Seller Awards und vielen Gelegenheiten, sich auszutauschen.

The sellers received 20 hours of eBay know-how as well as exclusive content on demand for 20 days. Almost 60 eBayers were involved in the production and organisation behind the scenes. Managers and team members took on different roles in front of the camera. This resulted in an informative and tailored programme: news broadcasts, talk shows, documentaries and reports behind the scenes. Prominent experts shared their eBay know-how in presentations and discussion rounds.

The participants were provided with their own channel for offering best practices and interactive sessions. They were able to converse with guests, take part in discussions and state their opinions in surveys. It was rounded off by an entertaining late-night show with a quiz, band, conferral of the Seller Awards and many opportunities to discuss with others.

BAYER CAPITAL MARKETS MEETING
ONLIVELINE GMBH – BÜRO FÜR KONZEPTION & INSZENIERUNG, COLOGNE

Location
BayComm, Leverkusen

Client
Bayer AG, Leverkusen

Month / Year
March 2021

Duration
Several days

Scenic direction
onliveline GmbH, Cologne

Show calling
Kate Addas, Berlin

Lighting
Jan-Christoph Hermann, Gründau

Media
insglück Gesellschaft für Markeninszenie-
rung mbH, Berlin

Others
Neumann & Müller GmbH & Co. KG,
Taufkirchen (Technological Conception and
realisation)

Photos
onliveline GmbH, Cologne

DYNAMISCHE KAMERA-BEWEGUNGEN UND EXKLUSIVE ORTE ERZEUGEN EINE PERSÖNLICHE ATMOSPHÄRE.

At the Capital Markets Meetings held by Bayer, the top management informs investors about the potential of the company. Due to the pandemic, it was not possible for these to take place live as usual, even though the company regards direct interaction as an important factor. The key task therefore consisted in transferring the personal atmosphere to a digital world. For onliveline, the location plays an important role in this: it must reflect the personality of the company. Their choice was therefore the Bayer Communication Center, a corporate brand space where it is possible to experience the umbrella brand and its products interactively as modern, with a lot of warmth and personality.

Bei den Capital Markets Meetings von Bayer informiert das Topmanagement die Investor:innen über das Potenzial des Unternehmens. Aufgrund der Pandemie konnten diese nicht wie gewohnt live stattfinden, obwohl der Konzern den direkten Austausch als wichtigen Faktor betrachtet. Die zentrale Aufgabe bestand somit darin, die persönliche Atmosphäre in die digitale Welt zu übertragen. Für onliveline spielt der Ort dabei eine wichtige Rolle: Er muss die Persönlichkeit des Unternehmens widerspiegeln. Die Wahl fiel daher auf das Bayer Communication Center, ein Corporate Brand Space, in dem man die Dachmarke und ihre Produkte modern, interaktiv und mit viel Wärme und Persönlichkeit erleben kann.

Dr. Ariane De Hoog
Moderation

Im Gegensatz zu der Idee, den Raum nur als Kulisse zu nutzen, entschied sich Bayer, stattdessen den gesamten Bereich mit seinen verschiedenen Ecken und Kuben mit einzubeziehen, um so jedem Mitglied des Teams einen individuellen Ort für seine Präsentationen zu geben. Auf diese Weise konnte das Online-Publikum den gesamten Brand Space erkunden. Moderator:innen führten in Begleitung einer beweglichen Kamera von einem Punkt zum anderen. Es entstand eine authentische, dynamische Umgebung, die durch die gemeinsame Bewegung durch den Raum ein vertrautes und persönliches Gefühl erzeugte.

Über eine dazugehörige gebrandete digitale Plattform konnten die Zuschauer:innen untereinander und mit dem Topmanagement interagieren und alle gezeigten Inhalte und Präsentationen erleben.

DYNAMIC CAMERA MOVEMENTS AND EXCLUSIVE LOCATIONS MAKE THE EVENT FEEL PERSONAL.

Contrary to the idea of only using the space as a setting, Bayer decided instead to incorporate the whole area with its various corners and cubes, in order to give each member of the team an individual place for their presentations. This allowed the online public to explore the whole brand space. A moderator provided guidance from one point to another, accompanied by a movable camera. This created authentic, dynamic surroundings with collective movement that generated a familiar and personal feeling throughout the space.

The spectators could interact with each other and with the top management through an accompaying branded digital platform and experience all the content and presentations shown.

Jede Zielgruppe hat unterschiedliche Bedürfnisse und Erwartungen. Dementsprechend sind Eventkonzepte im Idealfall nicht nur auf den Absender, sondern vor allem auf die Empfänger zugeschnitten.

FRIENDS: EIN EXKLUSIVER UND VOR ALLEM AUSGEWÄHLTER KREIS AN GÄSTEN, DER SICH AUS DEN UNTERSCHIEDLICHSTEN ZIELGRUPPEN ZUSAMMENSETZT: PARTNER, KUNDEN, FANS, WEGBEGLEITER, (LOKAL-)PROMINENZ, (BRANCHEN- UND UNTERNEHMENS-)VIPS, EHREN-GÄSTE UND MEDIENVERTRETER. TROTZ KULTURELLER UND GESELLSCHAFTLICHER HETERO-GENITÄT EINT SIE DIE TATSACHE, DASS SIE DEM GASTGEBER FREUNDSCHAFTLICH GESONNEN UND MEIST EINER DIREKTEN EINLADUNG GEFOLGT SIND.

Each target group has different requirements and expectations. Event concepts are therefore ideally not only geared towards the addressor, but especially towards the recipients.

FRIENDS: FRIENDS ARE AN EXCLUSIVE AND SELECTED CIRCLE OF GUESTS COMPOSED OF A WIDE RANGE OF TARGET GROUPS: PARTNERS, CUSTOMERS, FANS, COMPANIONS, (LOCAL) CELEBRITIES, VIPS (FROM COMPANIES AND THE SECTOR), GUESTS OF HONOUR AND MEDIA REPRESENTATIVES. DESPITE CULTURAL AND SOCIAL HETEROGENEITY, THEY ARE UNITED BY THE FACT THAT THEY ARE ON FRIENDLY TERMS WITH THE HOST AND MOSTLY RESPONDED TO A DIRECT INVITATION.

GOT2B MAKE-UP LAUNCH EVENT
STAGG & FRIENDS GMBH, DUSSELDORF

Location
Michelberger Hotel, Berlin

Client
Henkel AG & Co. KGaA, Dusseldorf

Month / Year
July 2021

Duration
1 day

**Dramaturgy / Direction / Coordination /
Architecture / Design / Graphics**
STAGG & FRIENDS GmbH, Dusseldorf

Lighting / Media / Filmss
cream digital pictures GmbH, Dusseldorf

Music
Wincent Weiss, Ana Kohler

Catering
Michelberger Hotel, Berlin

Construction
Artlife GmbH, Hofheim

Photos
*Schwarzkopf got2b, Dusseldorf;
cream digital pictures GmbH, Dusseldorf*

Für ein Make-up-Launch-Event der Marke Schwarzkopf got2b erschuf STAGG & FRIENDS ein zielgruppenaffines Konzept mit prägnantem Bühnendesign. Die Veranstaltung und ihr Setup ermöglichten individuelle Erlebnisse, Perspektiven und Inhalte für die geladenen Influencer:innen.

AN UNUSUAL VERTICAL SETUP THAT ALLOWS INDIVIDUAL PERSPECTIVES FOR INFLUENCERS.

For a makeup launch event for the brand Schwarzkopf got2b, STAGG & FRIENDS created a concept aimed at the target group with a striking stage design. The event and its setup allowed individual experiences, perspectives and content for the invited influencers.

The basis of the concept was the decentralised, colourful stage design, which was situated in the interior courtyard of a Berlin hotel. The surrounding rooms with a view of the interior courtyard became loges. Apart from the guests right by the stage, others followed the events live from the rooms and produced their own content from above. This resulted in various content streams running in parallel that achieved a wide reach into the relevant target group through the channels of the brand and the influencers.

EIN UNGEWOHN-TES, VERTIKALES SETUP, DAS INFLUENCER:INNEN INDIVIDUELLE PERSPEKTIVEN ERMÖGLICHT.

Grundlage des Konzepts war das dezentrale, farbenfrohe Bühnendesign. Es lag im Innenhof eines Berliner Hotels. Die umliegenden Zimmer mit Innenhofblick wurden zu Logen. Neben den Gästen direkt an der Bühne verfolgten andere das Geschehen live aus den Zimmern und produzierten eigenen Content von oben. So wurden verschiedene parallel laufende Content Streams erzeugt, die über die Kanäle der Marke sowie der Influencer:innen für Reichweite in die relevante Zielgruppe sorgten.

Während des Events wurden Besonderheiten der Make-up-Linie erklärt, die Beteiligten interviewt, das Produktdisplay enthüllt sowie Schminktipps von Make-up-Artistin Nina Park gegeben. Getreu dem Motto „Make-up is what you make of it" konnten sich alle an den Produkten bedienen und sie in einer lockeren Partyatmosphäre ausprobieren. Wie die Produkte selbst war das Essen überwiegend vegan und passte sich dem Zeitgeist an. Musikalische Untermalung boten Ana Kohler sowie Wincent Weiss als Highlight-Act.

Die größte Herausforderung des Events lag im Setup. Da es situationsbedingt ursprünglich überwiegend aus den Hotelzimmern verfolgt werden sollte, plante man die Gestaltung der Bühne vertikal statt horizontal und in 360 Grad. Kurzfristig konnten die Gäste auch live im Innenhof teilnehmen und das 3D-Setup optimal als Sitzmöglichkeit nutzen.

During the event, special features of the makeup line were explained, those involved were interviewed, the product display was revealed and makeup tips were provided by the makeup artist Nina Park. True to the motto "Makeup is what you make of it", everyone could help themselves to the products and try them out in a casual party atmosphere. Like the products themselves, the catering was primarily vegan and in keeping with the spirit of the times. Ana Kohler and Wincent Weiss as a highlight act provided the musical backdrop.

The greatest challenge of the event was posed by the setup. As it was originally supposed to be followed mainly from the hotel rooms due to the situation, the stage design was planned vertically instead of horizontally and at 360 degrees. At short notice, the guests were also able to participate live in the interior courtyard and take advantage of the optimal sitting provided by the 3D setup.

FRIENDS (CONCEPT)

THE SPHERE OF AMAZING
INSGLÜCK GESELLSCHAFT FÜR MARKEN-INSZENIERUNG MBH, BERLIN

Location
Corniche Boardwalk, Abu Dhabi

Client
Supreme Committee for Delivery & Legacy (SC), Doha

Month / Year
November 2020 (Reveal)

Duration
Until March 2023

Dramaturgy
insglück Frederik Nimmesgern, Cologne

Direction / Coordination
insglück Jessica Walheim, Cologne (Overall direction)

Architecture / Design
insglück Raed Caml, Berlin

Graphics
insglück David Tschechne / Juri Tschechne, Hamburg

Films
Elberfeld Kreation, Wuppertal

Photos
Renderings by insglück David Tschechne / Juri Tschechne, Hamburg

Vom 18. November bis 21. Dezember 2022 wird in Katar die 22. Ausgabe der FIFA Fussball-Weltmeisterschaft™ ausgetragen – die erste FIFA Fussball-Weltmeisterschaft in einem arabischen Land. Dementsprechend sollte die Countdown Clock von insglück nicht nur auf das sportliche Großevent einstimmen, sondern zugleich als erlebnisreicher Raum sowie als Bühne für erstaunliche Momente dienen.

Am 22. November 2020 sollte sie mit einer großen Eröffnungsveranstaltung eingeweiht, die Uhr symbolisch mit Emotionen aufgeladen und schließlich der Countdown gestartet werden. Ab der Aktivierung der Uhr waren regelmäßige PR-Events geplant, die das Bewusstsein für und die Vorfreude auf die FIFA Fussball-Weltmeisterschaft 2022 steigern sollten.

EINE COUNTDOWN CLOCK ALS BEGEH-BARER RAUM FÜR INSZENIERUNGEN, BEGEGNUNGEN UND EMOTIONEN.

The 22nd round of the FIFA World Cup will be held in Qatar from 18 November to 21 December 2022 – the first to take place in an Arabic country. In accordance with this, the Countdown Clock by insglück was intended not only to initiate the major sporting event but also serve as an eventful space and as a stage for extraordinary moments.

The inauguration was planned for 22 November 2020 with a large-scale opening event, associating the clock symbolically with emotions and then starting the countdown. After the activation of the clock, regular PR events were planned, designed to raise awareness and the anticipation of the FIFA World Cup 2022.

As the Sphere of Amazing is a space and not an object, it serves as a place where people meet and celebrate together. Placed on the Corniche, a symbolic location in Qatar, the clock becomes a visible landmark that represents an iconic and unique photo motif. During the competition, the giant clock can be used as a place for public viewings. After the last match of the FIFA World Cup 2022, the Countdown will be converted into a real clock.

Da es sich bei der Sphere of Amazing um einen Raum und nicht um ein Objekt handelt, wird sie zu einem Ort, an dem sich Menschen treffen und gemeinsam feiern. Platziert an der Corniche, einem symbolträchtigen Ort Katars, wird die Uhr zu einem sichtbaren Wahrzeichen, das ein ikonisches und einzigartiges Fotomotiv darstellt. Während des Turniers kann die riesige Uhr als ein Ort für Public Viewings genutzt werden. Nach dem letzten Spiel der FIFA Fussball-Weltmeisterschaft 2022 verwandelt sich der Countdown dann in eine echte Uhr.

A COUNTDOWN CLOCK AS A WALK-IN SPACE FOR STAGING, ENCOUNTERS AND EMOTIONS.

DACHSER – GENERAL LEADERSHIP MEETING 2021
ONLIVELINE GMBH – BÜRO FÜR KONZEPTION & INSZENIERUNG, COLOGNE

Location
bigBOX, Kempten

Client
Dachser Group SE & Co. KG, Kempten

Month / Year
March 2021

Duration
Several days

Dramaturgy / Direction / Coordination
onliveline GmbH, Cologne

Architecture / Design / Lighting
Jan-Christoph Hermann, Gründau

Media
Van De Space Maria und Tobias Düsing GbR, Berlin

Interactive floor projection
Frieder Weiss, Berlin

Music
Qosono GmbH & Co. KG, Neuss;
Matz Flores, Dusseldorf

Sound design
Matt Flores, Dusseldorf; Qosono GmbH & Co. KG, Neuss

Others
Qosono GmbH & Co. KG JC Hermann / Daniel Kaminski / Benjamin Schwenk, Neuss (Technical & Creative planning team); PRG Production Resource Group AG, Hamburg (Technological realisation)

Photos
onliveline GmbH, Cologne

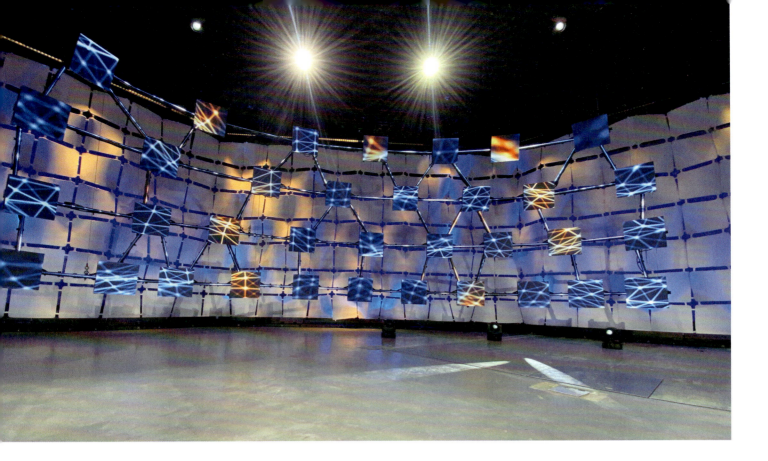

Die Agentur onliveline übernahm im März 2021 für DACHSER eine besondere Aufgabe: die Vorstellung des neuen CEO und seines Teams. Es galt, ein strategisches Storytelling zu entwickeln, das das neue Führungsteam nachhaltig und emotional präsentierte und zugleich über ein interaktives digitales Event den Anstoß für eine agilere Kultur gab.

Man entschied sich für fünf Settings, die in ihrem Narrativ die Werte der Familie mit dem operativen Geschäft und der Vision verbanden. Mit dynamischen Kamerabewegungen, szenischen Übergängen, medialen und speziellen Interaktions- und AR-Formaten inszenierten sie die Protagonist:innen in einem jeweils individuellen Kontext. Eine interaktive Plattform schuf einen zentralen gemeinsamen Rahmen.

AN EMOTIONAL, DYNAMIC PRESENTATION OF THE NEW MANAGEMENT TEAM AND THE FUTURE CULTURE.

The agency onliveline took on a special task for DACHSER in March 2021: the introduction of the new CEO and his team. It was about developing strategic storytelling that presented the new management team memorably and emotionally and at the same time provided the impetus for a more agile culture through an interactive digital event.

EINE EMOTIONALE, DYNAMISCHE INSZENIERUNG DES NEUEN FÜHRUNGS-TEAMS UND DER KÜNFTIGEN KULTUR.

Am Abend wurden die Standorte und das Netzwerk ge-würdigt – mit einer emotional inszenierten Preisverleihung einschließlich interaktiver Bodenprojektion und dem in den Raum übertragenen Applaus der digitalen Gäste.

Am zweiten Tag fokussierte sich das Event auf die Zukunft und die neuen strategischen Wege. Präzise inszenierte Persönlichkeiten, Interaktionen, strategische Settings und die Auseinandersetzung mit der Zukunft wurden zum Start-schuss für einen ganzheitlichen Kommunikationsprozess.

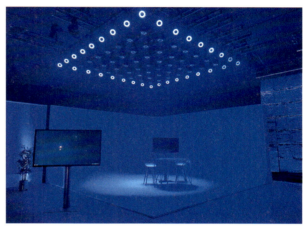

They decided on five settings that brought together family values, the operative business and the vision in their nar-rative. With dynamic camera movements, scenic transitions, media and special interaction and augmented reality for-mats, they set the scene for the protagonists in respective individual contexts. An interactive platform provided a central shared framework.

In the evening, the locations and the network were ho-noured – with an emotionally staged prize award, includ-ing an interactive floor projection and the applause of the digital guests transmitted into the space.

On the second day, the event focussed on the future and the new strategic paths. Personalities presented in detail, interactions, strategic settings and considerations of the future provided the impetus for a comprehensive commu-nication process.

THE UNCONVENTIONAL EXPERIENCE –
A BRAND ONBOARDING
STAGG & FRIENDS GMBH, DUSSELDORF

Location
*Tegernsee surroundings / Hotel Bussi Baby,
Bad Wiessee*

Client
*Active Nutrition International GmbH |
Powerbar, Munich*

Month / Year
August 2021

Duration
3 days

**Dramaturgy / Direction / Coordination /
Architecture / Design / Decoration**
STAGG & FRIENDS GmbH, Dusseldorf

Graphics
Rapid Peaks GmbH, Munich

Catering
HOTEL BUSSI BABY GmbH, Bad Wiessee

Others
*Active Nutrition International GmbH,
Munich (Handling of influencers
and athletes)*

Photos
*Active Nutrition International GmbH,
Munich; Rapid Peaks GmbH, Munich*

EINE SPORTLICHE SCHNITZELJAGD STELLT DIE NEUE MARKENSTRATEGIE ALS SPIELERISCHES ERLEBNIS VOR.

Influencers and athletes were to be involved in the communication at an early stage for the brand relaunch of Powerbar in the year 2022. In order to convey information surrounding the "new Powerbar" in a fun manner and gather material for the brand campaign, STAGG & FRIENDS developed the Unconventional Experience – a sporty scavenger hunt. The participants got to know the brand playfully amidst nature, instead of at a staged location.

Für den Marken-Relaunch von Powerbar im Jahr 2022 sollten Influencer:innen und Athlet:innen frühzeitig in die Kommunikation einbezogen werden. Um Informationen rund um das „neue Powerbar" mit Spaß zu vermitteln und Material für die Markenkampagne zu sammeln, entwickelten STAGG & FRIENDS die Unconventional Experience – eine sportliche Schnitzeljagd. Anstatt in einer inszenierten Location lernten die Teilnehmer:innen die Marke mitten in der Natur und auf spielerische Art kennen.

A SPORTY SCAVENGER HUNT INTRODUCES THE NEW BRAND STRATEGY AS A PLAYFUL EXPERIENCE.

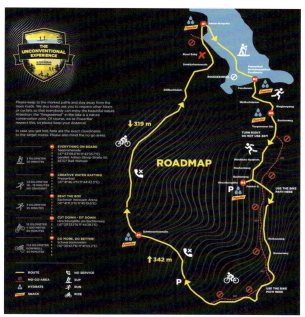

Als Orientierungssystem leiteten Pfeile, eine Map und die App Komoot die Mitmachenden durch das Gelände. An verschiedenen Stationen erhielt jede Gruppe verrückte Aufgaben, die im Team zu lösen waren und die neue Marken-DNA erlebbar werden ließen. Die Wege zwischen den Stationen wurden für Shootings genutzt. Fortbewegt wurde sich Rad fahrend, joggend und stehpaddelnd quer über den Tegernsee. Zusätzlich erhielt jede Gruppe Videochallenges, die über Telegram mit der Jury und den anderen Gruppen geteilt werden sollten.

Im Ziel angekommen erhielten die Teilnehmer:innen Einblick in die neue Markenstrategie. Der Punktestand der einzelnen Gruppen definierte das Setup für das anschließende Abendevent. Das bei dem gemeinsamen Erlebnis entstandene Bildmaterial wurde fester Bestandteil der nachfolgenden Powerbar-Kampagne.

Arrows, a map and the Komoot app guided the participants through the terrain as an orientation system, as they moved by bike, jogging or stand-up paddling across the lake Tegernsee to various stations, where each group was given crazy tasks to be solved as a team and to turn the new brand DNA into an experience. The paths between the stations were used for photo shoots. In addition, each group received video challenges that they were supposed to share with the jury and the other groups through the telegram channel.

Upon arrival at the end, the participants were given an insight into the new brand strategy. The score of the individual groups defined the setup for the concluding evening event. The visual material resulting from the shared experience became an integral component of the ensuing Powerbar campaign.

COUNTDOWN CLOCK LAUNCH
FISCHERAPPELT, LIVE MARKETING GMBH, COLOGNE

Location
Fishing Spot at the Doha Corniche, Doha

Client
*Supreme Committee for Delivery & Legacy
(SC), Doha*

Month / Year
November 2021

Duration
1 day

Awards
*Gold at Golden Award of Montreux 2022
(Celebration / Anniversary)*

Dramaturgy
*fischerAppelt, live marketing GmbH,
Cologne; Hans-Christoph Mücke, Bielefeld;
Tobias Stupeler, Rösrath*

Direction / Coordination
Harry Seedorf, Berlin

Architecture / Design
imagination, Doha

Graphics / Lighting
bright! GmbH, Maintal

Media / Films / Decoration / Construction
*fischerAppelt, live marketing GmbH,
Cologne*

Music
smg music production, Münster

Artists / Show acts
International Doha communities

Photos
*Supreme Committee for Delivery & Legacy
(SC), Doha*

ENTHÜLLUNG DER FIFA WORLD CUP COUNTDOWN CLOCK – EINDRUCKS-VOLL UND MOTIVIE-REND INSZENIERT.

A countdown symbol was originally already supposed to be installed two years before the FIFA World Cup 2022 in Qatar. This was repeatedly postponed due to the pandemic, until around eight weeks before the unveiling a new briefing was issued to the handling agency fischerAppelt. All the preparations, the media production for the show, the animations, music composition and dramaturgy had to be realised in less than four weeks. The countdown clock was finally ceremoniously unveiled on 11 / 21 / 21 at a live event with 150 invited VIP guests and streamed broadcasting.

Ursprünglich sollte schon zwei Jahre vor der FIFA Fussball-Weltmeisterschaft™ 2022 in Katar ein Countdown-Symbol installiert werden. Durch die Pandemie wurde dies mehrfach verschoben, bis etwa acht Wochen vor der Enthüllung ein neues Briefing an die betreuende Agentur fischerAppelt gegeben wurde. Alle Vorbereitungen, Medienproduktion für die Show, Animationen, Musikkomposition und Dramaturgie mussten in weniger als vier Wochen realisiert werden. Bei einer Live-Veranstaltung mit 150 geladenen VIP-Gästen und gestreamtem Broadcasting wurde die Countdown Clock letztlich am 21.11.21 feierlich enthüllt.

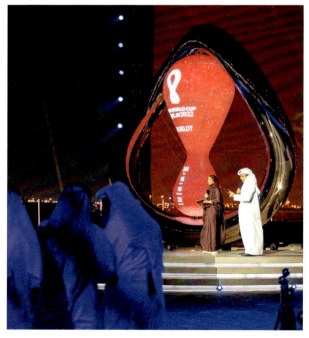

The basic idea consisted of a motivating speech aimed by a coach in the changing room – as it turned out – not only at a football team but a whole nation: Appealing to the people in Qatar and beyond. At the end of his "locker room speech", the coach started up a beat for the people in Qatar to join into.

Die Grundidee bestand in einer motivierenden Rede, die ein Coach in der Umkleidekabine – wie sich herausstellte – nicht nur an ein Fußballteam richtete, sondern an eine ganze Nation: Die Menschen in Katar und darüber hinaus sollten angesprochen und bewegt werden. Der Coach initiierte am Ende seiner „locker room speech" einen Beat, in den die Menschen in Katar einsetzen sollten.

Das Setting wurde mit freier Sicht über das Wasser zur Doha-Skyline konzipiert. Um der Kamera und auch den Gästen einen Ausblick darauf zu erlauben, wurde für die Projektion ein Screen aus transparentem Showtex-Material genutzt. Der Content wurde so produziert, dass aus allen Perspektiven ein einheitliches Bild entstand. Die Countdown Clock selbst war unter einer Stoffplane verdeckt und wurde im Rahmen einer Drohnenshow über der Skyline von Doha mittels eines Kabuki-Systems effektvoll enthüllt.

The setting was designed with an open view across the water towards the Doha skyline. In order to allow both the camera and the guests a view of it, a screen made of transparent ShowTex material was used for the projection. The content was produced to form a uniform image from all perspectives. The countdown clock itself was covered by a fabric sheet and was revealed to great effect as part of a drone show over the Doha skyline by means of a kabuki system.

UNVEILING OF THE FIFA WORLD CUP COUNTDOWN CLOCK – IN AN IMPRESSIVE AND MOTIVATING SETTING.

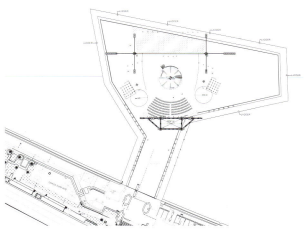

Jede Zielgruppe hat unterschiedliche Bedürfnisse und Erwartungen. Dementsprechend sind Eventkonzepte im Idealfall nicht nur auf den Absender, sondern vor allem auf die Empfänger zugeschnitten.

PRESS: SÄMTLICHE VERTRETER DER MEDIEN, ALSO NATIONALE UND INTERNATIONALE JOURNALISTEN (TV, PRINT, RADIO), BLOGGER, INFLUENCER – ALL JENE MULTIPLIKATOREN, DIE DAS SUJET BEHERRSCHEN UND INHALTE GEKONNT WEITERTRAGEN SOLLEN. DASS BEI DIESER ZIELGRUPPE LIVEKOMMUNIKATION AN ERSTER STELLE STEHT, IST SELBSTVERSTÄNDLICH ...

Each target group has different requirements and expectations. Event concepts are therefore ideally not only geared towards the addressor, but especially towards the recipients.

PRESS: ALL REPRESENTATIVES OF THE MEDIA, NATIONAL AND INTERNATIONAL JOURNALISTS (TV, PRINT, RADIO), BLOGGERS, INFLUENCERS – ALL THE DISSEMINATORS WHO MASTER THE SUBJECT AND CAN SPREAD CONTENT EXPERTLY. IT GOES WITHOUT SAYING THAT LIVE COMMUNICATION IS KEY WITH THIS TARGET GROUP ...

BEYERDYNAMIC PRO X LAUNCH EVENT
BRUCE B. CORPORATE COMMUNICATION GMBH, STUTTGART; 0711 LIVECOM GMBH, STUTTGART

Location
Online

Client
beyerdynamic GmbH & Co. KG, Heilbronn

Month / Year
October 2021

Duration
2 days (plus 1 month accessibility),
1.5 hour event in 3 time zones

**Dramaturgy / Direction / Architecture /
Design / Graphics**
*Bruce B. corporate communication GmbH,
Stuttgart*

Coordination
0711 Livecom GmbH, Stuttgart

Development
b.ReX GmbH, Stuttgart

Photos
*Bruce B. corporate communication GmbH,
Stuttgart*

Pandemiebedingt sollte ein zuerst für eine Messe geplanter Produktlaunch von beyerdynamic umgedacht werden. Bruce B. und 0711 überzeugten das Unternehmen von einem digitalen Presseevent und entwickelten einen eigenständigen, virtuellen 360-Grad-Markenraum. In der Pre-Event-Phase, zirka zwei Wochen vor dem Launch, öffnete er seine digitalen Tore mit einem Countdown. Die Produkte und Informationen blieben jedoch noch verhüllt und nicht sichtbar.

EIN VIRTUELLER PRODUKTLAUNCH MIT EIGENSTÄNDIGEM, DIGITALEM 360-GRAD-MARKENRAUM.

A VIRTUAL PRODUCT LAUNCH WITH AN INDEPENDENT, DIGITAL, 360-DEGREE BRAND SPACE.

Due to the pandemic, a product launch by beyerdynamic originally planned for a trade fair had to be rethought. Bruce B. and 0711 convinced the company to go ahead with a digital media event and developed an independent, virtual, 360-degree brand space. In the pre-event phase, about two weeks before the launch, it opened its digital gates with a countdown. However, the products and information still remained concealed and not visible.

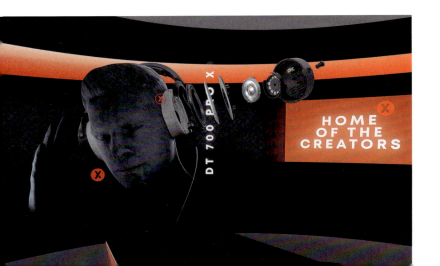

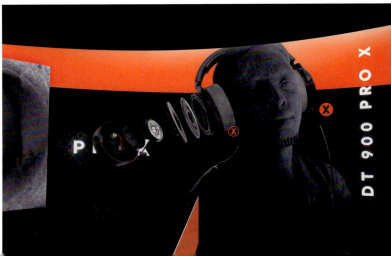

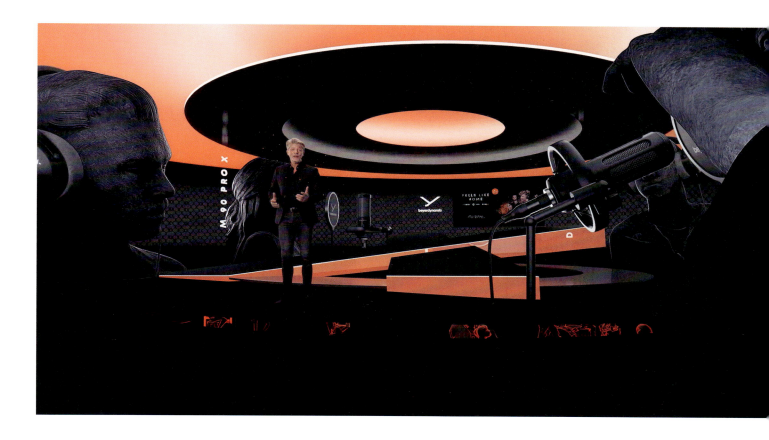

Mit Ablauf des Countdowns „erschien" der CEO von beyerdynamic als holografischer Film und begrüßte die digitalen
Gäste. Die darauf folgende Enthüllung der Produkte wurde
mithilfe von Explosions-Animationen inszeniert und von
vertiefenden Informationsebenen begleitet.

Der virtuelle Produktlaunch war parallel in drei Zeitzonen
verfügbar, der Markenraum mit Produkten und Inhalten
über mehrere Wochen präsent. Nicht zuletzt stellte die
Kampagne die Produkte sowie die Menschen dahinter
persönlich vor. Entwickelt und umgesetzt wurde die Anwendung auf Basis der agentureigenen digitalen Veran-
staltungsplattform MUNIS.

At the end of the countdown, the CEO of beyerdynamic
"appeared" as a holographic film and welcomed the digital
guests. The subsequent reveal of the products was staged
with the help of explosion animations and accompanied by
more in-depth information.

The virtual product launch was available in three time
zones at once, and the brand space with its products and
contents was present for several weeks. The campaign
presented not only the products but also the people behind them in person. The application was developed and
realised on the basis of the agency's own digital event
platform MUNIS.

THE LÄND PRESS CONFERENCE UMBRELLA BRAND EVENT
MILLA & PARTNER GMBH, STUTTGART;
JUNG VON MATT NECKAR GMBH, STUTTGART

Location
Stuttgart Harbour

Client
State Ministry Baden-Württemberg, Stuttgart

Month / Year
October 2021

Duration
1 day (Press conference); ongoing

Dramaturgy / Direction / Coordination / Architecture / Design
Milla & Partner GmbH, Stuttgart

Graphics / Films
Jung von Matt NECKAR GmbH, Stuttgart

Lighting
music & light design GmbH, Leonberg

Media
music & light design GmbH, Leonberg (Media technology); Jung von Matt NECKAR GmbH, Stuttgart (Media feed)

Music
Klangerfinder GmbH & Co KG, Stuttgart; Jung von Matt NECKAR GmbH, Stuttgart

Decoration
Milla & Partner GmbH, Stuttgart; Stadelmayer Werbung GmbH, Kirchheim/Teck

Catering
Luchterhand Bio-Catering, Stuttgart

Construction
Stadelmayer Werbung GmbH, Kirchheim/Teck

Photos
Günther Bayerl, Neu-Ulm

EINE PRESSE-KONFERENZ SETZT DIE PRÄGNANTE IMAGEKAMPAGNE MIT POP-UP-TOUR IN SZENE.

Jung von Matt NECKAR and MILLA & PARTNER developed a new image campaign in order to attract (inter)national professionals to Baden-Württemberg and to communicate topics such as innovation, progress, economic strength, environment, humanity, as well as quality of life and enjoyment. It was designed to draw international attention and create recognition value. The result was "Baden-Württemberg. THE LÄND". It was intended to be humorous and serious at the same time – modest, self-ironic and especially memorable. The stated goal was for "THE LÄND" to become everyday language, expressing the diversity of the federal state.

Um (inter-)nationale Fachkräfte für Baden-Württemberg zu begeistern und Themen wie Innovation, Fortschritt, Wirtschaftskraft, Umwelt, Menschlichkeit sowie Lebensqualität und Genuss zu kommunizieren, entwickelten Jung von Matt NECKAR und MILLA & PARTNER eine neue Imagekampagne. Sie sollte internationale Strahlkraft und Wiedererkennungseffekte erzeugen. Entstanden ist: „Baden-Württemberg. THE LÄND". Humorvoll und ernst gemeint zugleich – uneitel, selbstironisch und vor allem merkfähig. Erklärtes Ziel ist, dass „THE LÄND" in den Sprachgebrauch übergeht und die Vielseitigkeit des Bundeslandes zum Ausdruck kommt.

Vorgestellt wurde die neue Dachmarkenkampagne in einer Pressekonferenz am Stuttgarter Hafen. Eine ideale Kulisse, die sowohl an einem wichtigen Verkehrsknotenpunkt mit industriellem Umschlagplatz als auch vor den Weinbergen und Streuobstwiesen des Neckartals liegt. In einem modernen Setting aus Europaletten, LED-Screens und (grafischen) Querverweisen auf den Ort kamen Akteur:innen aus Politik und Wirtschaft zu Wort.

Effektvoll inszeniert wurde während der Konferenz auch der nächste Baustein der Kampagnen-Lancierung: Ein Greifstapler hob den mobilen Shop aus der Taufe, der künftig Teil einer landesweiten Pop-up-Tour ist. Im Übersee-Container sind THE LÄND-Merchandising-Artikel – von Badges bis zu T-Shirts und Hoodies – zu kaufen, die aus Baden-Württemberg-Fans Botschafter:innen des Landes machen sollen. Mit der neuen Dachmarke sind weitere nationale und internationale Aktionen und Beteiligungen an Events und Messen geplant.

A PRESS CONFERENCE HIGHLIGHTS THE STRIKING IMAGE CAMPAIGN WITH A POP-UP TOUR.

The new umbrella brand campaign was presented at a press conference at Stuttgart port, an ideal setting that lies both at an important transport hub with an industrial reloading point and in front of the vineyards and meadow orchards of the Neckar Valley. Protagonists from politics and economics had their say in a modern setting with euro-pallets, LED screens and (graphic) references to the location.

The next building block of the campaign launch was also staged to great effect during the conference: a reach stacker lifted the mobile shop that will be part of the nationwide pop-up tour in future. THE LÄND merchandising articles – from badges to T-shirts and hoodies – are available for purchase in the overseas container, designed to make Baden-Württemberg fans ambassadors of the state. Further (inter)national campaigns and participation in events and trade fairs are planned with the new umbrella brand.

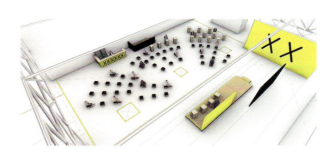

MERCEDES-BENZ PRE-NIGHT IAA 2021
OLIVER SCHROTT KOMMUNIKATION GMBH, COLOGNE

Location
Mercedes-Benz Dealership, Munich

Client
Mercedes-Benz AG, Stuttgart

Month / Year
September 2021

Duration
1 day

Dramaturgy / Architecture / Design / Graphics / Films
Oliver Schrott Kommunikation GmbH, Cologne

Direction / Coordination
Dirk Ludwig; Andree Verleger; Oliver Schrott Kommunikation GmbH, Cologne

Lighting
IXPI GmbH, Cologne; Sound & Light Veranstaltungstechnik GmbH, Leonberg

Media
wsmp.tv GmbH, Berlin; Capture Media GmbH, Dusseldorf; AV-X GmbH, Oststeinbek

Music
Idee und Klang, Basel; amp Music, Berlin

Artists / Show acts
Adelinde Knorr Showdesign, Munich; DEVADO

Construction
tec ViSiON GmbH, Frankfurt am Main; Klartext GmbH, Willich

Photos
Oliver Schrott Kommunikation GmbH, Cologne; Mercedes-Benz AG, Stuttgart

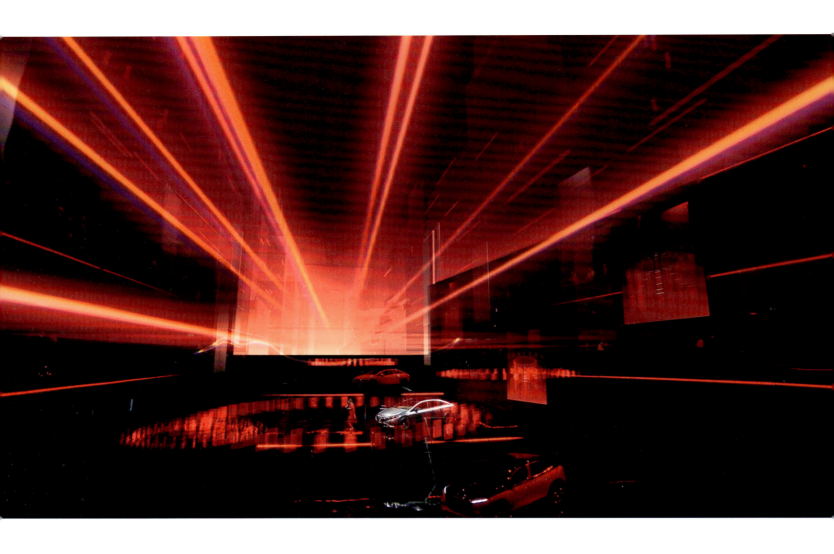

EIN DIGITALES LIVE-ERLEBNIS SPIELT MIT PHYSISCHEN UND DIGITAL AUGMENTIERTEN KULISSEN.

Nach anderthalb Jahren ohne physische Messen bot die IAA MOBILITY 2021 für Mercedes-Benz die Chance, ein hybrides Event zu realisieren: Die Premiere von vier elektrischen Fahrzeugen sollte sowohl das Publikum vor Ort in München als auch auf der ganzen Welt ansprechen.

Gemeinsam mit dem Medienkünstler Andree Verleger verwirklichte OSK ein neuartiges Event, das analog und digital Zuschauende gleichermaßen begeistern sollte. In diesem Sinne spielte das Markenerlebnis gezielt mit den Grenzen physischer Elemente – und bot dem digitalen Publikum eine exklusive Perspektive.

After a year and a half without physical trade fairs, IAA MOBILITY 2021 offered Mercedes-Benz the opportunity to realise a hybrid event: the premiere of four electric vehicles was designed to appeal to the public both locally in Munich and around the world.

Together with the media artist Andree Verleger, OSK realised a novel event that was intended to enthuse analogue and digital spectators alike. With this in mind, the brand experience played with the limits of physical elements in a targeted manner and offered the digital public an exclusive perspective.

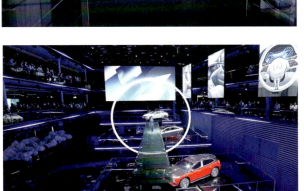

3D worlds were created on the livestream specifically for each of the four vehicles with the help of live augmented reality content. While the public in Munich was following the real show, for the digital spectators the physical experience blended with the digitally augmented 3D setting. This created a novel and exclusive venue for the online participants.

Im Livestream wurden mithilfe von Live-Augmented-Reality-Inhalten eigene 3D-Welten für jedes der vier Fahrzeuge entwickelt. Während das Publikum in München die reale Show verfolgte, verschmolz das physische Erlebnis für die Zuschauer:innen an den Bildschirmen mit der digital augmentierten 3D-Kulisse. So entstand für die online Teilnehmenden ein neuartiger und exklusiver Ort.

A DIGITAL LIVE EXPERIENCE PLAYS WITH PHYSICAL AND DIGITALLY AUGMENTED SETTINGS.

Jede Zielgruppe hat unterschiedliche Bedürfnisse und Erwartungen. Dementsprechend sind Eventkonzepte im Idealfall nicht nur auf den Absender, sondern vor allem auf die Empfänger zugeschnitten.

EMPLOYEES: MITARBEITER EINES ODER MEHRERER UNTERNEHMEN, DIE ZUMEIST MOTIVIERT, ZUSAMMEN-GESCHWEISST ODER GRUND-SÄTZLICH BESSER GESTIMMT WERDEN SOLLEN. DIESE ZIELGRUPPE BEDARF EINES BESONDEREN FEINGEFÜHLS, UM DIE ZIELVORGABEN DES MANAGEMENTS MIT DER EMOTIONALEN WAHRNEHMUNG DER MITARBEITER ZU VEREIN-BAREN UND DIE BEABSICHTIGTE BOTSCHAFT ZU KOMMUNIZIEREN.

Each target group has different requirements and expectations. Event concepts are therefore ideally not only geared towards the addressor, but especially towards the recipients.

EMPLOYEES: EMPLOYEES FROM ONE OR MORE COMPANIES WHO ARE USUALLY TO BE MOTIVATED, BROUGHT TOGETHER OR GENERALLY HAVE THEIR SPIRITS RAISED. THIS TARGET GROUP REQUIRES A SPECIAL TOUCH IN ORDER TO ALIGN THE AIMS OF THE MANAGEMENT WITH THE EMOTIONAL PERCEPTION OF THE EMPLOYEES AND TO COMMUNICATE THE INTENDED MESSAGE.

C:ONFERENCE 1.21 – TIME TO TRANSFORM
MUTABOR BRANDSPACES GMBH, HAMBURG

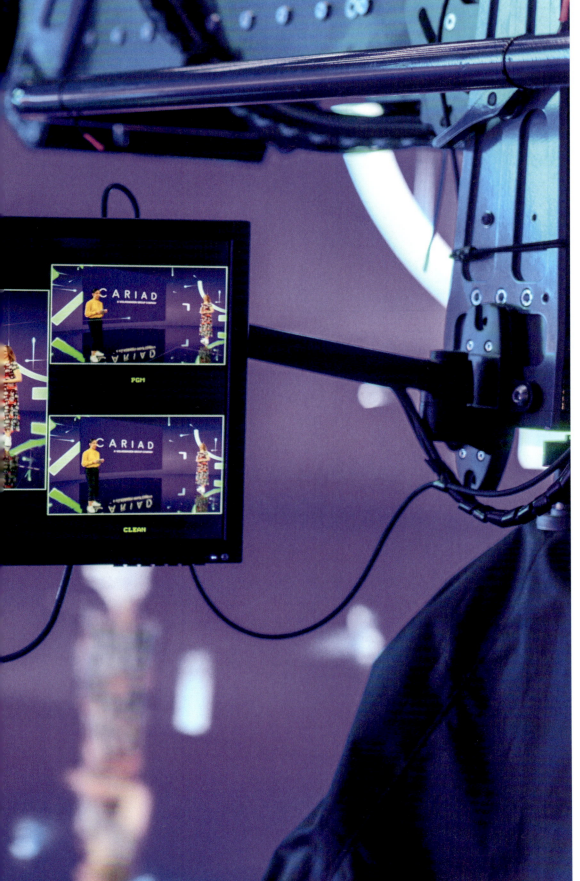

Location
Online / HYPERBOWL Studio, Munich (Production)

Client
CARIAD SE, Wolfsburg

Month / Year
March 2021

Duration
90 minutes

Dramaturgy / Direction / Coordination / Architecture / Design
MUTABOR Brandspaces GmbH, Hamburg

Graphics
MUTABOR Brandspaces GmbH, Hamburg; FAKTOR 3 AG, Hamburg (Presentation)

Lighting / Media
HYPERBOWL GmbH, Munich

Films
Awesome Pixels GmbH & Co. KG, Blaustein (Post production); MUTABOR Brandspaces GmbH, Hamburg

Artists / Show acts
Jennifer Sarah Boone (Moderator)

Others
NSYNK Gesellschaft für Kunst und Technik mbH, Frankfurt am Main (Virtual studio, AR); movingimage EVP GmbH, Berlin (Stream); Protofy GmbH & Co. KG, Hamburg (App development)

Photos
Knoth Fotografie Kai-Uwe Knoth, Langenhagen

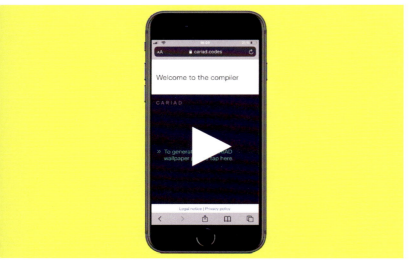

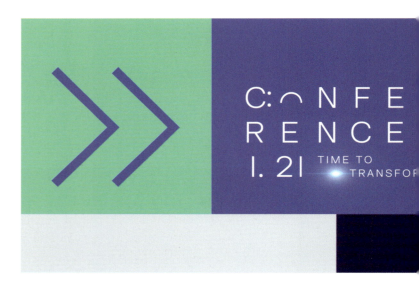

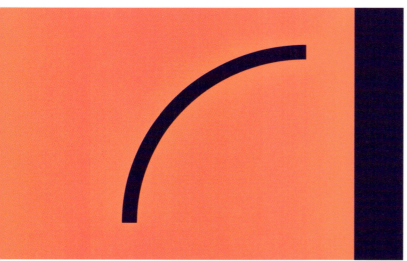

EIN DIGITALES LAUNCH-EVENT – MIT VIRTUELLEN, REALEN UND INTERAKTIVEN KOMPONENTEN.

Software development is the driving topic in the mobility industry. For this reason, from now on the Volkswagen Group is consolidating the necessary competences in a new company named CARIAD SE. A symbolic framework was to be developed for the launch under the motto "Time to transform", presenting the corporate design and the name. The content was designed to target the employees and their emotions.

Software-Entwicklung ist das treibende Thema der Mobilitätsbranche. Aus diesem Grund bündelt der Volkswagen Konzern fortan die Kompetenzen in einer neuen Marke mit dem Namen CARIAD SE. Für den Launch unter dem Motto „Time to transform" sollte ein symbolträchtiger Rahmen entwickelt werden, der das Corporate Design und den Namen präsentiert. Mitarbeiter:innen sollten inhaltlich abgeholt und emotional eingestimmt werden.

A DIGITAL LAUNCH EVENT – WITH VIRTUAL, REAL AND INTERACTIVE COMPONENTS.

MUTABOR gestaltete eine Veranstaltung im Virtual-Pro-
duction-Studio in der Hyperbowl in München. In einem Mix
aus virtueller und realer Welt gingen das neue Corporate
Design und der neue Name gemeinsam mit 4000 Mitarbeitenden an den Bildschirmen live. Das Programm des Events
war durch AR-Elemente angereichert und beinhaltete interaktive Komponenten. Ein Höhepunkt: Die Mitarbeiter:innen
hatten die Möglichkeit, ihren Namen über das Smartphone
einzugeben, der dann im virtuellen Raum der Veranstaltung
für alle sichtbar im neuen CD erschien und den oder die
Angestellte:n als Teil der CARIAD-Familie präsentierte.

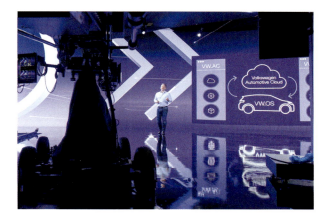

MUTABOR designed an event at the Virtual Production
Studio in the Hyperbowl in Munich. The new corporate
design and the new name, together with 4000 employees,
went live on the screens with a mix of virtual and real worlds.
The event programme was enriched by augmented reality
elements and included interactive components. A highlight:
the employees had the possibility to enter their name via
smartphone, which then appeared in the virtual space of
the event for all to see and presented the employee as part
of the CARIAD family.

FUJITSU EMPLOYEE CEE KICK-OFF 21
HEAD OF EVENT GMBH, DUSSELDORF

Location
Palladium, Cologne

Client
Fujitsu Technology Solutions GmbH, Munich

Month / Year
April 2021

Duration
2 days

Dramaturgy
Dr. Carl Naughton, Wiesbaden;
HEAD OF EVENT GmbH Cheryl Martinez,
Dusseldorf

Direction / Coordination
HEAD OF EVENT GmbH Markus Dresen,
Dusseldorf

Graphics / 3D Animation
Gecko Grafik Roman Plötzer, Dusseldorf

Films
FORMAT54 Lennart Schinke, Cologne

Photos
Tilo Wandelt Fotografie, Cologne

Wie können im Rahmen einer zentralen Mitarbeiterveran-
staltung neue Strategien platziert, verinnerlicht und erlebbar gemacht werden? Wie können sich Mitarbeitende trotz
Corona-Beschränkungen treffen und in Kontakt bleiben?
HEAD OF EVENT beantwortete diese Fragen für Fujitsu
mit einem eigenständigen, auf die Kundenanforderungen
zugeschnittenen Live-TV-Sender.

AN INTERACTIVE AND ENTERTAINING LIVE TV FORMAT – BY AND FOR THE EMPLOYEES.

EIN INTERAKTIVES UND UNTERHALTSAMES LIVE-TV-FORMAT – VON UND FÜR DIE MITARBEITENDEN.

How can new strategies be launched, internalised and
turned into an experience during a major internal event?
How can colleagues meet and stay in touch despite corona
restrictions? HEAD OF EVENT answered these questions
for Fujitsu with a live TV broadcast exactly tailored to the
customer's needs.

In collaboration with Dr. Carl Naughton, a wide-ranging concept was developed. An editorial team put together content for more than 15 programmes. At the same time, Fujitsu employees were given plenty of room to realise their own ideas with professional support. The result was, for instance, late-night formats with music and live songs, tablet tennis, Pong and a "whisper challenge" for charity. The programme was densely packed and completely live: from game shows and talks with management to the latest news – all realised in a variety of settings.

A custom-designed interactive platform enabled smooth access to the up to five parallel streams and chat rooms with surveys and open exchange. After the event, contributions from both days were still available to employees on demand.

In Zusammenarbeit mit Dr. Carl Naughton wurde ein Konzept mit großer Bandbreite entwickelt. Ein Redaktionsteam stellte Inhalte für mehr als 15 Programme zusammen. Gleichzeitig gab man den Fujitsu-Mitarbeiter:innen viel Raum, ihre eigenen Ideen mit professioneller Unterstützung zu gestalten. So entstanden unter anderem Late-Night-Formate mit Musik und Live-Gesang, Tablet-Tennis, Pong und eine Whisper-Challenge für den guten Zweck. Das Programm war dicht gepackt und komplett live: von Gameshows über Talks mit dem Management bis hin zu den aktuellsten News – alle realisiert in unterschiedlichen Settings.

Eine eigens gestaltete Plattform ermöglichte einen reibungslosen Zugriff auf die bis zu fünf parallelen Streams und Chaträume mit Umfragen und freiem Austausch. Die vielseitigen Beiträge beider Tage standen den Mitarbeiter:innen auch nach dem Event on demand zur Verfügung.

MERCEDES-BENZ GLOBAL TRAINING EXPERIENCE CITAN 2021

STAGG & FRIENDS GMBH, DUSSELDORF

Location
XPOST Köln, Cologne

Client
Mercedes-Benz Global Training, Stuttgart

Month / Year
September / October 2021

Duration
6 weeks (24 hours per participant)

Dramaturgy
art.of.us – creative works, Cologne

Direction / Coordination
STAGG & FRIENDS GmbH, Dusseldorf

Architecture / Design / Media / Films
jangled nerves GmbH, Stuttgart

Lighting
PRG Germany, Hamburg

Decoration / Construction
Artlife GmbH, Hofheim

Catering
Kofler & Kompanie Newco GmbH, Berlin

Photos
teamfoto Marquardt, Lüdingshausen

AKTIVIERENDE LERNERLEBNISSE MIT GAMIFICATION UND AUTHENTISCHEN TESTFAHRTEN.

Mit der Global Training Experience Citan 2021 war ein internationales Trainingsevent für 4000 Teilnehmende der Mercedes-Benz Vans Vertriebsmannschaft geplant. Die Agentur STAGG & FRIENDS übernahm die Betreuung und realisierte ein coronakonformes, abwechslungsreiches Training in Köln. Mit einem maßgeschneiderten Hygienekonzept erstreckte sich das Event über sechs Wochen und ermöglichte es den Teilnehmer:innen, für jeweils 24 Stunden in eine eigens geschaffene Marken- und Produktwelt einzutauchen.

An international training event for 4000 members of the Mercedes-Benz Vans sales team was planned with the Global Training Experience Citan 2021. The agency STAGG & FRIENDS took over its handling and realised a varied training experience in Cologne with a tailored hygiene concept in compliance with coronavirus regulations. The event spanned six weeks and allowed the participants to immerse themselves for 24 hours respectively into a specially created brand and product world.

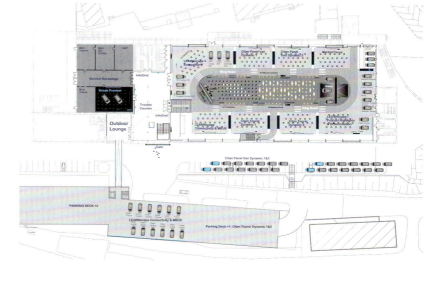

ACTIVATING LEARNING EXPERIENCES WITH GAMIFICATION AND AUTHENTIC TEST DRIVES.

Der Claim der Marketingkampagne – „The all-new Mercedes-Benz Citan – FEELS GIANT" – stand Pate bei der Ausgestaltung des Trainingscampus. Neben Testfahrten im Zielgruppenumfeld des neuen Citan standen aktivierende Lernerlebnisse im 4000 Quadratmeter großen LEARNscape im Vordergrund.

Die myGTEApp diente mit Blick auf das Hygienekonzept zur Steuerung der Kontakte, Abläufe und Timings. Zugleich unterstützte sie auch beim Lernen: Digitale Trainings-Touchpoints sollten mit Gamification-Elementen komplexe Produktinhalte spielerisch vermitteln. Das Hands-on-Training erfolgte für die Teilnehmenden mit verschiedensten digitalen Aufgabenstellungen sowie direkt auf dem eigenen Mobile Device. Die Möglichkeit, in der GTE-Challenge Punkte zu sammeln, schuf zusätzliche Anreize.

"The all-new Mercedes-Benz Citan – FEELS GIANT" – the claim of the marketing campaign was the inspiration for the design of the training campus. Apart from test drives for the target group surrounding the new Citan, the focus was on activating learning experiences in the 4000-square-metre LEARNscape.

The myGTEApp served the purpose of managing contacts, processes and timing, with a view to the hygiene concept. It also supported learning, with digital training touchpoints designed to playfully convey complex product content with gamification elements. The hands-on training for the participants was by means of a wide variety of digital tasks and directly on their own mobile device. The possibility of gathering points in the GTE challenge provided additional impetus.

EUNITED 2021
UNIPLAN GMBH & CO. KG, COLOGNE

Location
Bright Studios of bright! gmbh, Maintal

Client
Michelin Reifenwerke AG & Co. KGaA, Karlsruhe

Month / Year
*January – September 2021
(Virtual Kick-Off, Main Event, Follow-Ups)*

Duration
9 months (5 days for events)

Graphics
Carsten Mell, Rösrath (Superheroes illustration)

Photos
Uniplan GmbH & Co. KG, Cologne

A DIGITAL EVENT SERIES ALLOWS EMPLOYEES TO PARTICIPATE IN CHANGES WITHIN THE COMPANY.

Wie kommuniziert man ein internes 500-Millionen-Euro-Einspar- und Transformationsprogramm und motiviert 1500 Mitarbeiter:innen in zehn Ländern, diesen Wandel mitzugehen? Und das auf rein digitalem Weg? Eine komplexe Aufgabe, mit der sich Uniplan im Auftrag von Michelin Ende 2020 auseinanderzusetzen hatte. Ihr inhaltlicher Ansatz: Man aktiviert die Superkräfte eines jeden Mitarbeitenden und verwandelt sie in Helden, die den Umbruch selbst mitgestalten.

How does one communicate an internal 500-million-euro savings and transformation programme and motivate 1500 employees in ten countries to go along with this change? And on purely digital channels at that? Uniplan faced this complex task on behalf of Michelin at the end of 2020. Their approach in terms of content was to activate the superpowers of every employee and turn them into heroes who help to shape the transformation.

EINE DIGITALE VERANSTALTUNGS-REIHE LÄSST MITARBEITENDE DEN FIRMENWANDEL MITGESTALTEN.

Mit „Michelin EUNited 2021" wurde über neun Monate hinweg eine fünfstufige digitale Employee Journey kreiert, durch die das Unternehmen und die Michelin Region Nordeuropa mittels Co-Construction umgestaltet werden sollten. Auf Grundlage psychologischer Theorien über menschliches Verhalten im Change-Management und den Stufen der „Heldenreise" konzipierte und produzierte die Agentur eine Reihe digitaler Veranstaltungen, die die Mitarbeitenden aktiv in den Veränderungsprozess einband.

Den Anfang machte eine Videobotschaft des Managements, die die Menschen zunächst mit dem beängstigenden Wandel konfrontierte. Es folgte ein umfassendes Angebot interner Tools und Inhalte, die den Dialog miteinander und letztlich die Akzeptanz des Wandels fördern sollte. Höhepunkt der Veranstaltungsreihe war eine zweitägige digitale Konferenz mit mehr als 30 internen Redner:innen und über 1300 Teilnehmenden. Sie diente als Plattform des Ideenaustauschs, bot verschiedene Formate und schaffte ein informatives wie auch unterhaltsames Erlebnis. Die Ergebnisse wurden in zwei Folgeveranstaltungen vorgestellt, diskutiert und waren die Basis für die neue Vision und Strategie des Unternehmens. Der Grundstein für die Zukunft wurde so gemeinsam gelegt.

With "Michelin EUNited 2021", a five-stage digital employee journey was created over a period of nine months, through which the company and the Michelin region of Europe North were to be restructured by means of co-construction. On the basis of psychological theories of human behaviour in change management and the steps of the "hero journey", the agency created and produced a series of digital events that helped employees become an active part of the change process.

A video message by the management at the start confronted the employees with the alarming change. This was followed by a comprehensive offer of internal tools and content intended to encourage dialogue and ultimately acceptance of the change. The highlight of the transformation journey was a two-day digital conference with more than 30 internal speakers and over 1300 participants. It served as a platform for sharing ideas, offered various meetings and created an informative and entertaining experience. The results were presented and discussed in two follow-up events and provided the basis for the company's new vision and strategy. The foundations for the future were thus laid together.

Jede Zielgruppe hat unterschiedliche Bedürfnisse und Erwartungen. Dementsprechend sind Eventkonzepte im Idealfall nicht nur auf den Absender, sondern vor allem auf die Empfänger zugeschnitten.

EXPERTS: FACHPUBLIKUM, BRANCHENKENNER UND EXPERTEN, DIE AN EINEM GEMEINSAMEN THEMA INTERESSIERT SIND. DER AUSTAUSCH AUF FACHEBENE STEHT DABEI IM MITTELPUNKT UND PRÄGT DIE KOMMUNIKATION WESENTLICH. DIESE ZIELGRUPPE IST VORNEHMLICH AN DER VERMITTLUNG VON WISSEN INTERESSIERT, DIE WEIT ÜBER DIE WEITERGABE REINER INFORMATIONEN HINAUSGEHT.

Each target group has different requirements and expectations. Event concepts are therefore ideally not only geared towards the addressor, but especially towards the recipients.

EXPERTS: THESE ARE A SPECIALIST PUBLIC AND EXPERTS IN THE SECTOR WHO ARE INTERESTED IN A COMMON SUBJECT. THE FOCUS IS ON AN EXCHANGE AT EXPERT LEVEL, WHICH SHAPES THE COMMUNICATION SIGNIFICANTLY. THIS TARGET GROUP IS PRIMARILY INTERESTED IN THE TRANSMISSION OF KNOWLEDGE THAT GOES WAY BEYOND THE PASSING ON OF MERE INFORMATION.

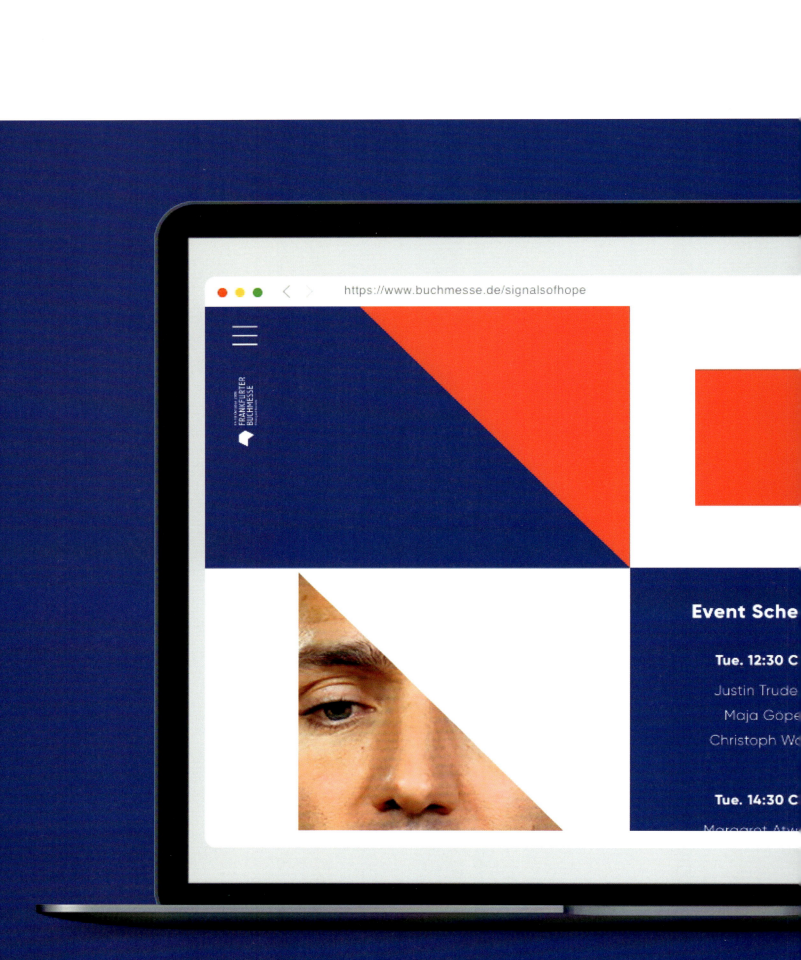

https://www.buchmesse.de/signalsofhope

FRANKFURTER BUCHMESSE

Event Sche

Tue. 12:30 C

Justin Trude

Maja Göpe

Christoph Wo

Tue. 14:30 C

Margaret Atw

SIGNALS OF HOPE
FISCHERAPPELT, LIVE MARKETING GMBH, COLOGNE

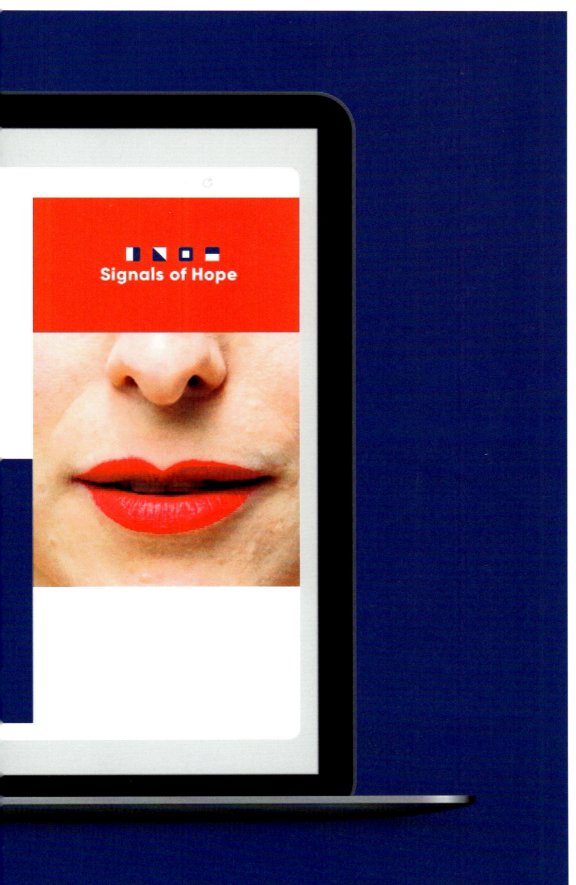

Location
Frankfurt Book Fair, Frankfurt am Main / Spreegraphen Studios, Berlin (Production)

Client
Frankfurter Buchmesse GmbH, Frankfurt am Main

Month / Year
October 2020

Duration
5 days

Awards
Silver (Best Digital Event) and Bronze (Best Format Events) at BrandEx 2022; Gold at Golden Award of Montreux 2021 (Online / Hybrid Events); ADC 2021 (Corporate Event); PR Report Award (Event and Live Communication)

Dramaturgy
fischerAppelt, live marketing GmbH, Cologne

Direction / Coordination / Architecture / Design / Films / Artists / Show acts
fischerAppelt, live marketing GmbH, Cologne; Fork Unstable Media GmbH, Hamburg

Graphics
Fork Unstable Media GmbH, Hamburg

Lighting
AMBION Veranstaltungstechnik GmbH, Berlin

Media
fischerAppelt, relations GmbH, Hamburg; Fork Unstable Media GmbH, Hamburg

Decoration / Construction
Deko-Service Lenzen GmbH, Lohmar

Catering
Berlin Cuisine Jensen GmbH, Berlin

Photos
fischerAppelt, live marketing GmbH, Cologne

Erderwärmung, globale Ungerechtigkeit, der Kampf um Gleichberechtigung: Im Jahr 2020 erschien die Zukunft ungewisser denn je. Die Frankfurter Buchmesse wollte im Krisenjahr 2020 das Potenzial des „Prinzips Hoffnung" aufzeigen und „Signals of Hope" senden – nicht nur an den von der Corona-Krise gebeutelten Kultur- und Literaturbetrieb, sondern an die ganze Welt. Mit diesem Anspruch wurde mit fischerAppelt ein digitales Podiumevent entwickelt, über das Persönlichkeiten aus Gesellschaft und Literatur eine Plattform bekamen, um Perspektiven aufzuzeigen und Lösungen zu erarbeiten.

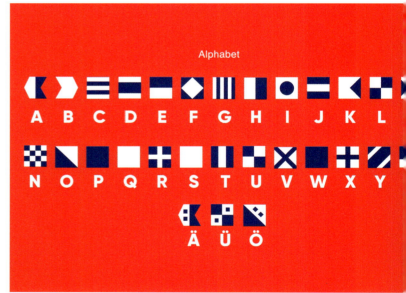

Global warming, globa injustice, the fight for equal rights: In the year 2020, the future appeared more uncertain than ever. In this crisis year, the Frankfurt Book Fair wanted to show the potential of the "principle of hope" and send "signals of hope" – not only to the fields of culture and literature stifled by the corona crisis but also to the whole world. With this aim in mind, a digital podium event was developed with fischerAppelt, giving prominent personalities from society and literature a platform for presenting perspectives and formulating solutions.

EIN DIGITALES PODIUMEVENT SENDET MIT PRÄGNANTER BILDSPRACHE UND VIELSEITIGEM PROGRAMM HOFFNUNG.

The first digital and international event of the Frankfurt Book Fair was thus created in accordance with the key idea of "signals of hope". It was a corona-resistant concept and at the same time a special edition for the Book Fair 2020. The programme content was respectful and international with well thought out variety.

In their choice of design, the agency drew on a communication method that also serves the safety of human life and communication over long distances: the international signal alphabet. This resulted in a distinctive and playful pictorial language that presented the varied programme consistently and strikingly – and could be taken up and spread by influencers.

A DIGITAL PODIUM EVENT SENDS HOPE WITH A DISTINCTIVE PICTORIAL LANGUAGE AND A VARIED PROGRAMME.

Unter der Leitidee „Signals of Hope" entstand damit das erste digitale und internationale Event der Frankfurter Buchmesse. Ein coronaresistentes Konzept und zugleich eine Special Edition für die Buchmesse 2020. Das inhaltliche Programm wurde bewusst vielfältig, respektvoll und international gestaltet.

In der Wahl des Designs griff die Agentur auf eine Kommunikationstechnik zurück, die ebenfalls der Sicherheit von Menschenleben und zur Kommunikation über große Distanzen hinweg dient: das internationale Signalalphabet. So entstand eine prägnante und verspielte Bildsprache, die das vielfältige Programm konsistent und auffällig präsentierte – und von Multiplikatoren aufgegriffen und verbreitet werden konnte.

SAP NOW GERMANY
INSGLÜCK GESELLSCHAFT FÜR MARKEN-INSZENIERUNG MBH, BERLIN

Location
Alte Schildkrötfabrik, Mannheim

Client
SAP Deutschland SE & Co. KG, Walldorf

Month / Year
March 2021

Duration
2 days

Dramaturgy
*insglück Tobias Bergmann, Cologne;
Tobias Stupeler, Cologne*

Direction / Coordination
*insglück Kim Detlefsen, Hamburg
(Overall direction); Jan-Erik Stahl, Hamburg
(Programme direction)*

Graphics
insglück Janina Quante, Cologne

Media
insglück Alexander Rose, Berlin

Artists / Show acts
*Dr. Anne Gfrerer (Moderator);
Scherer Werbung GmbH, Stuttgart (Speaker
management)*

Decoration
*BALLONI GmbH, Berlin;
Katrin Hampus, Munich (Set design)*

Construction
*epicto GmbH, Edingen-Neckarhausen
(Technical supplier); plazz AG, Erfurt
(Platform); TFN GmbH & Co. KG, Hamburg
(Technical direction)*

Others
*insglück Clarissa Majerus / Franziska
Nebelin / Lana Fast / Malte Heindl / Nadine
Mönnich, Cologne & Hamburg (Partial
direction, Project management)*

Photos
*Carina C. Kircher Businessfotografin.de,
Heidelberg – Berlin*

Zeit, neu zu denken

SAP NOW Germany
09. – 10. März 2021

EIN INTERAKTIVER DIGITALER CONTENT-HUB MIT 18 STUNDEN LIVE-PROGRAMM FÜR DIE SAP-COMMUNITY.

Unter dem Motto „Zeit, neu zu denken" fand 2021 das Online-Event SAP NOW Germany statt. Hierfür gestaltete insglück einen interaktiven und abwechslungsreichen Content Hub rund um die Themen neue Technologien, digitale Transformation, Trends und Wissenstransfer für die SAP-Community.

The online event SAP NOW Germany took place in 2021 under the motto "Time to rethink". For this, insglück created an interactive and varied content hub based on topics around new technologies, digital transformation, trends and knowledge transfer for the SAP community.

The two-day event offered a live programme totalling 18 hours – with five talk magazines, 51 interactive breakout sessions and eight showcases. The formats were based on three focal points: inspiring outlooks (Inspire), in-depth insights (Explore) and interactive exchanges (Connect).

Die zweitägige Veranstaltung bot insgesamt 18 Stunden Live-Programm – mit fünf Talkmagazinen, 51 interaktiven Breakout-Sessions und acht Showcases. Die Inhalte basierten dabei auf drei Format-Schwerpunkten: inspirierende Ausblicke (Inspire), vertiefende Einblicke (Explore) und interaktiver Austausch (Connect).

Als besonderes Feature ermöglichte der sogenannte NOW-O-MAT jedem der mehr als 3500 Teilnehmenden ein individuell auf sie oder ihn zugeschnittenes Programm. Insgesamt stand neben der Vielzahl an Inhalten das intuitive Netzwerken zwischen SAP-Expert:innen, Kund:innen und Partnern im Mittelpunkt des Geschehens.

As a special feature, the so-called NOW-O-MAT allowed each of the more than 3500 participants an individually tailored programme. Apart from the variety of content, the focus of the event was on intuitive networking between SAP experts, customers and partners.

AN INTERACTIVE DIGITAL CONTENT HUB WITH A LIVE PROGRAMME TOTALLING 18 HOURS FOR THE SAP COMMUNITY.

OPEN UP NEW DIMENSIONS – HYBRID ONCOLOGY LAUNCH
ONLIVELINE GMBH – BÜRO FÜR KONZEPTION & INSZENIERUNG, COLOGNE

Location
TMT Studios Munich (Production)

Client
Daiichi Sankyo Europe, Munich

Month / Year
November 2021

Duration
Several days

Dramaturgy / Direction / Coordination
onliveline GmbH, Cologne

Graphics
Regiepapst Medienproduktion GmbH, Munich (+ Unreal gaming technology); Stefan Gunkel, Baden-Baden (VR room design)

Films
Van De Space Maria und Tobias Düsing GbR, Berlin; Filmproduktion Peter Schüttemeyer, Cologne

Music
Qosono GmbH & Co. KG Hansjörg Wenzel, Neuss

Construction
Michael Blatzheim DUGFEM e. K., Röthenbach an der Pegnitz

Others
ARTHUR TECHNOLOGIES INC., Taiwan (VR space); onliveline GmbH, Cologne & N+B IT GmbH, Schwelm (Platform); Jan Tellenbach IXPI GmbH, Cologne (Technical direction)

Photos
onliveline GmbH, Cologne

EPISODE 1
What's UP?
Time travellers logbook -
11th March 2021 4pm

EPISODE 2
Look UP!
Time travellers logbook -
1st December 1910 10:12 am

EPISODE 3
Stand UP!
Time travellers logbook -
11th March 2011 2:22 pm

EPISODE 4
Speed UP!
Time travellers logbook -
28th March 1922 7:30 pm

EPISODE 5
Team UP!
Time travellers logbook -
23rd February 2014 3 pm

EPISODE 6
It's UP to US!
Time travellers logbook -
3rd April 1830 6 pm

Für den Hybrid Oncology Launch Ende 2021 entwickelte onliveline ein Konzept, das die Markteinführung als ganzheitliche, interaktive Geschichte erzählte. Dabei wurde Takeko, eine Samurai-Kriegerin, in sechs Episoden zur Protagonistin der Vorkommunikation. Auf einer Online-Plattform verfolgte sie die Entstehung eines neuen Wirkstoffs, der die Krebsbehandlung revolutionieren soll, und erzählte die Geschichte der vielen Held:innen, die an dieser neuen Technologie arbeiten. Die Vorkommunikation sollte alle Mitarbeitenden zusammenbringen, um etwas über die Mission zu erfahren. Interaktionen sollten initiiert, Grußkarten verschickt und das Kennenlernen über Speed-Datings in wonder.me angeregt werden.

For the Hybrid Oncology Launch at the end of 2021, onliveline developed a concept that narrated the market launch as a comprehensive, interactive story. Takeko, a Samurai warrioress, became the protagonist of the preparatory communication in six episodes. On an online platform, she traced the development of a new substance that was supposed to revolutionise cancer treatment and told the story of the many heroes and heroines working on this new technology. The advance communication was intended to bring all those involved together to find out about the mission, to initiate interactions, send greeting cards and to encourage encounters through speed dating on wonder.me.

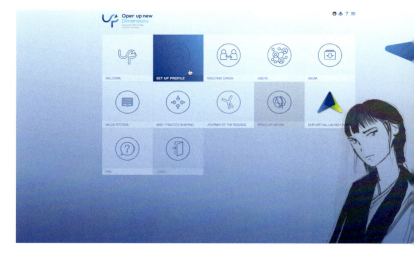

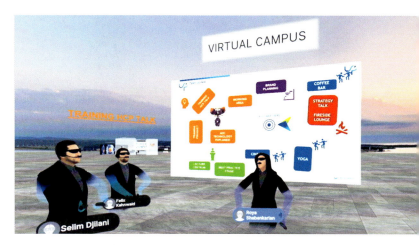

EIN PRODUKT-LAUNCH, DER ALS INSZENIERTE UND INTER-AKTIVE GESCHICHTE NACHHALTIG WIRKEN SOLL.

Im März kamen schließlich fast 300 Mitarbeiter:innen online unter dem Motto „Open up new Dimensions" zusammen. Das hybride Launch-Event kombinierte virtuelle und reale Settings mit der Unreal-Gaming-Technologie und bezog VR-Elemente ein. Den Start bildete ein binaurales Hörspiel, das Bilder in den Köpfen der Teilnehmenden erzeugen sollte.

In the end, almost 300 employees came together online in March under the motto "Open up new Dimensions". The hybrid launch event combined virtual and real settings with unreal gaming technology and incorporated virtual reality elements. A binaural audio play formed the start, designed to evoke images in the minds of the participants.

Daiichi leaders from all around the world provided insights into the strategy, immersed themselves in the new technology and the manufacturing process and ensured that all the employees were on the right track. Breakout sessions provided the opportunity to develop ideas and to consider how everyone wished to work in their European team. In the end, it was Takeko again who handed over her logbook to all the employees. After the launch event, the participants could continue to write the story and stay in contact on the online platform.

Daiichi-Führungskräfte aus aller Welt gaben Einblicke in die Strategie, vertieften sich in die neue Technologie und den Herstellungsprozess und stellten sicher, dass alle Mitarbeiter:innen auf dem richtigen Weg waren. Breakout-Sitzungen gaben die Möglichkeit, Denkweisen zu entwickeln und zu überlegen, wie jeder in seinem europäischen Team arbeiten wollte. Am Ende war es wieder Takeko, die allen Mitarbeitenden ihr Logbuch überreichte. Nach der Auftaktveranstaltung konnten die Teilnehmer:innen die Geschichte weiterschreiben und auf der Online-Plattform in Verbindung bleiben.

A PRODUCT LAUNCH DESIGNED TO HAVE A LASTING EFFECT AS A STAGED AND INTER-ACTIVE STORY.

MARC CAIN FASHION FILM "KEEP ON DANCING" SPRING / SUMMER 2022
MARC CAIN GMBH, BODELSHAUSEN

Location
Marc Cain Headquarters, Bodelshausen

Client
Marc Cain GmbH, Bodelshausen

Month / Year
July 2021

Duration
Debut at Digital Fashion Week, permanent on YouTube and Social media

Dramaturgy / Direction / Coordination
Marc Cain GmbH, Bodelshausen

Lighting
Willi Rätzsch, Stuttgart

Films
Pat Borriello, Stuttgart

Artists / Show acts
Eric Gauthier (Choreography); Luis Sayago (Assistant); Evelyn Tatiana Martinez, Danielle Marie Bezair, Yi-wei Tien (Dancers)

Others
Olga Pashchievska, Zen Zhang (Models)

Photos
Katja and Fabian Madzar, Stuttgart

Many digital formats were developed also in the fashion industry due to the pandemic, including the trade fair format "Digital Fashion Week – Europe" that took place in summer 2021. Marc Cain presented its spring collections 2022 as part of this – with the specially produced film "Keep on Dancing".

A DIGITAL FASHION FILM PREMIERE AND ANALOGUE DANCE PERFORMANCES PRESENT THE NEW COLLECTION.

Auch in der Modebranche haben sich pandemiebedingt viele digitale Formate entwickelt. Darunter das Messeformat „Digital Fashion Week – Europe", das im Sommer 2021 stattfand. Marc Cain präsentierte in diesem Rahmen seine Frühjahrskollektionen 2022 – mit dem eigens produzierten Film „Keep on Dancing".

Passend zum Saisonmotto präsentierte der gleichnamige Fashion Film mit tänzerischer Leichtigkeit die Marc Cain-Kollektionen, neue Silhouetten sowie die Exklusivität der Materialien. Dabei wurde das Marc Cain Headquarter zur Tanzbühne. Die Choreografie stammt von dem international erfolgreichen Tänzer und Choreografen Eric Gauthier.

Der Film feierte auf der Mainstage der „Digital Fashion Week – Europe" seine Premiere und wurde anschließend auf dem YouTube-Channel und den weiteren Social-Media-Kanälen von Marc Cain veröffentlicht. Während der Erstausstrahlung auf der Messeplattform hatten die Zuschauer:innen die Möglichkeit, sich via Chatfunktion direkt mit Marc Cain auszutauschen. Choreografierte Live-Dance-Performances auf den Straßen in Düsseldorf (während der DFD), Berlin (während der Fashion Week), New York (während der COTERIE) und Barcelona führten den „Keep on Dancing"-Gedanken weiter.

In keeping with the season's motto, the fashion film of the same name presented the Marc Cain collections, new silhouettes and the exclusivity of materials with playful dance. The Marc Cain headquarters were turned into a dance stage. The choreography comes from the internationally successful dancer and choreographer Eric Gauthier.

The film celebrated its premiere on the main stage of the "Digital Fashion Week – Europe" and was then published on Marc Cain's YouTube and other social media channels. During the first broadcast on the exhibition platform, the spectators had the opportu-nity to converse directly with Marc Cain via a chat function. Choreographed live dance performances on the streets of Dusseldorf (during the DFD), Berlin (during Fashion Week), New York (during COTERIE) and Barcelona kept the "Keep on Dancing" idea going.

EINE DIGITALE FASHION-FILM-PREMIERE UND ANALOGE DANCE-PERFORMANCES PRÄSENTIEREN DIE NEUE KOLLEKTION.

ELEVATION DIGITAL DAYS
UNIPLAN GMBH & CO. KG, COLOGNE

Location
Elegant Elephant Studio / VOSS TV Studio, Dusseldorf

Client
Vodafone GmbH, Dusseldorf

Month / Year
April 2021

Duration
3 days

Awards
Red Dot Design Award 2021; Gold at German Brand Award 2022 (Excellence in Brand Strategy and Creation – Branded Activities During COVID-19)

Direction / Coordination
Chris Cuhls, Cologne; Konstanze Agatz, Berlin; Stephan Bolz, Hanover

Lighting / Media
Aventem GmbH, Hilden

Catering
Dein Speisesalon, Cologne

Others
Dexper, Amsterdam (Platform)

Photos
NEUARTIG FILM Matthias Heuser, Krefeld

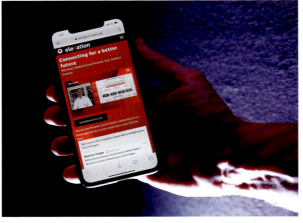

A DIGITAL CON-FERENCE COMBINES CONTENT, A BRAND PRESENTATION AND CUSTOMER CONTACTS.

Vodafone präsentiert seinen Geschäftskunden eigene Projekte, Innovationen und Konzepte üblicherweise bei regelmäßig stattfindenden Konferenzen. Aufgrund der Pandemie jedoch konnten diese nicht wie gewohnt stattfinden. Deshalb sollte Uniplan ein alternatives Konzept entwickeln, das die Attraktivität einer traditionellen Konferenz mit einem digitalen User- und Content-Erlebnis verbindet und zugleich potenzielle Kunden anzieht.

Vodafone usually presents its own projects, innovations and concepts to business partners at regularly held conferences. However, these could not take place as usual due to the pandemic. Uniplan was therefore tasked with developing an alternative concept that combines the attractiveness of a traditional conference w th a digital user and content experience and at the same time draws potential customers.

Nach einem Jahr Vorbereitung veranstaltete Vodafone Business im April 2021 die Premiere der eleVation DIGITAL DAYS 2021 in Düsseldorf. Die COVID-konforme digitale Konferenz bot über drei Tage hinweg 195 Referent:innen auf drei Bühnen, 48 Keynotes und 59 Deep Dives. Daraus ergaben sich mehr als 70 Stunden meist simultan gedolmetschter Inhalte, die live gestreamt und später als Video-on-Demand zur Verfügung gestellt wurden.

EINE DIGITALE KONFERENZ VERBINDET CONTENT, MARKENPRÄSENTATION UND KUNDENKONTAKTE.

Ein robustes Streaming und eine eigene digitale Eventplattform stellten sicher, dass alle Nutzer:innen, unabhängig von ihrer verfügbaren Bandbreite und über mehrere Streams hinweg, problemlos teilhaben konnten. Mehr als 15.000 Menschen registrierten sich. Zu den belebtesten Zeiten waren 7000 auf der Plattform aktiv.

After a year of preparation, Vodafone Business held the premiere of eleVation DIGITAL DAYS 2021 in Dusseldorf in April 2021. The digital conference that conformed to COVID regulations offered 195 speakers on three stages, 48 keynotes and 59 deep dives over a period of three days. This resulted in more than 70 hours of mostly simultaneously interpreted content, which was streamed live and made available later as video-on-demand.

Robust streaming and a dedicated digital event platform ensured that all the users could take part easily, regardless of their available bandwidth and across several streams. More than 15,000 people registered. At the busiest times, 7000 were active on the platform.

HHS – HAMBURG HEMOPHILIA SYMPOSIUM
ONLIVELINE GMBH – BÜRO FÜR KONZEPTION & INSZENIERUNG, COLOGNE

Location
DAS CORVATSCH, Munich

Client
Takeda Pharma Vertrieb GmbH & Co. KG, Berlin

Month / Year
November 2021

Duration
Several days

Dramaturgy
onliveline GmbH, Cologne

Direction / Coordination
onliveline Petra Lammers, Cologne;
expopartner GmbH, Flörsheim am Main

Architecture / Design / Lighting
Jan-Christoph Hermann, Gründau

Graphics / Decoration
expopartner GmbH, Flörsheim am Main

Media
Van De Space Maria und Tobias Düsing GbR, Berlin

Music
Matz Flores, Dusseldorf

Technology
Limelight, Breisach am Rhein

Construction
expopartner GmbH, Flörsheim am Main (Agency)

Others
onliveline GmbH, Cologne (onIT Platform);
Qosono GmbH & Co. KG JC Hermann /
Daniel Kaminski / Benjamin Schwenk (Technical & Creative planning team)

Photos
onliveline GmbH, Cologne

Das zweitägige, digitale Hämophilie-Symposium mit durchweg komplexen Fachinhalten spannend zu gestalten, ist schon an sich eine Herausforderung. Im November 2021 kam noch hinzu, dass es das zweite digitale Symposium war: Die gleichen Gäste. Die gleiche Location. Die gleichen Gastgeber. Und: Die grundsätzlich gleiche Struktur. Unter dieser Prämisse wählte onliveline einen neuen Ansatz und machte aus der Veranstaltung eine Erzählung.

A SYMPOSIUM BECOMES A FICTITIOUS FLAT SHARE AND A STORY WITH A VARIETY OF PARTICIPATORY ACTIVITIES.

EIN SYMPOSIUM WIRD ZUR FIKTIVEN WG UND EINER GESCHICHTE MIT VIELSEITIGER TEILHABE.

Fiktiver Schauplatz war die WG der beiden Gastgeber: Ärzte und Experten zum Thema Hämophilie. Sie und ihr „Hausgast" begrüßten die Gäste und Referent:innen bei sich zu Hause. Die „Überwachungskameras" zeigten in Schwarz-Weiß die Wohnung, während die „Gastkameras" sich neugierig und in Farbe durch die WG bewegten, sich umschauten und Teil der Diskussion waren. Jede Diskussion endete mit Take Home Messages, die aus dem Digitalen von den Untermietern ausgedruckt und dem Hausgast überbracht wurden.

Über eine Plattform konnten die Gäste mit den Gastgebern interagieren, Postkarten in die WG schicken, mit den Referent:innen diskutieren, applaudieren und interaktiv an diversen Formaten teilnehmen. Zu heiklen Themen gab es ein Pro-und-Contra-Battle, an dem sich alle beteiligen konnten. Zur Veranstaltung gehörten darüber hinaus eine Posterausstellung sowie diverse Awards.

Making the two-day digital haemophilia symposium with its complex specialist content interesting is a challenge in itself. Furthermore, in November 2021 it was the second digital symposium: with the same guests, the same location, the same hosts and basically the same structure. With this in mind, onliveline took a new approach and turned the event into a narrative.

The fictitious scene was the flat share of the two hosts: doctors and experts who presented the topic of haemophilia. They and their "house guest" greeted the guests and speakers at their home. The "monitoring cameras" showed the flat in black and white, while the "guest cameras" moved through the flat curiously and in colour, looking around and becoming part of the discussion. Every discussion ended with take home messages, which were printed out from the digital version by the subtenants and provided to the house guest.

The guests could interact with the hosts through a platform, send postcards to the flat share, discuss with the speakers, applaud and take part interactively in various formats. There was a for and against battle regarding hot topics, which everyone could participate in. The event also included a poster exhibition and various awards.

JUNG LOVES ... EXHIBITION OF THINGS
RAUMKONTOR INNENARCHITEKTUR, DUSSELDORF

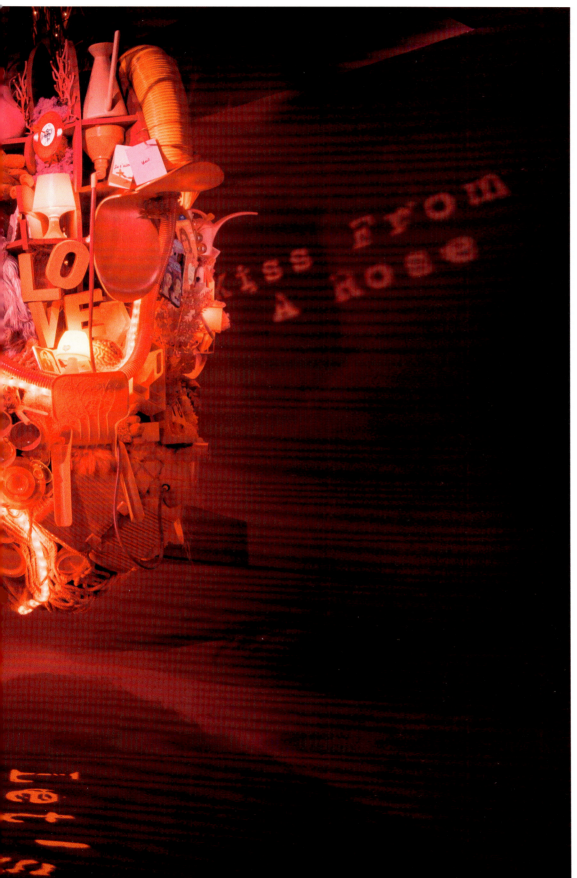

Location
Ballet studio, Milan

Client
*Albrecht Jung GmbH & Co. KG,
Schalksmühle*

Month / Year
September 2021 (Fuorisalone)

Duration
Several days

Dramaturgy / Architecture / Design
*raumkontor Innenarchitektur Andrea Weitz /
Prof. Jens Wendland, Dusseldorf*

Direction / Coordination
*Albrecht Jung GmbH & Co. KG Deniz Turgut /
André Klauke / Dijane Slavic, Schalksmühle;
raumkontor Innenarchitektur, Dusseldorf*

Graphics
Panorama Betzler Bork Roth GbR, Stuttgart

Lighting / Media
Jan Hördemann, Essen

Decoration
Angelika Vienken, Dusseldorf

Construction
standex GmbH, Wuppertal

Photos
*bildhübsche fotografie | Andreas Körner,
Stuttgart*

EINE KÜNSTLERISCHE, PULSIERENDE SKULPTUR VERMITTELT DIE LIEBE ZU ARCHITEKTUR UND DESIGN.

Der Gebäudetechnik-Anbieter JUNG präsentierte sich im Jahr 2021 auf dem Mailänder Fuorisalone. Im Rahmen dieses Auftritts sollte der Claim „JUNG loves architecture" mit einer emotionalen, unverwechselbaren und erinnerbaren Installation kommuniziert werden. Die Kreativen von raumkontor entwickelten mit diesem Ziel die Ausstellung „JUNG LOVES ... Exhibition of Things".

The building technology supplier JUNG presented itself in the year 2021 at the Fuorisalone in Milan. The aim of this presentation was to communicate the claim "JUNG loves architecture" by means of an emotional, distinctive and memorable installation. With this in mind, the creative team at raumkontor developed the exhibition "JUNG LOVES ... Exhibition of Things".

The dramaturgic concept first enticed the visitors out of the Milan sunshine and into the exhibition area with a deep heartbeat. A dark, magical space awaited them there with pulsating sound, moving text projections, colours and the central exhibition object.

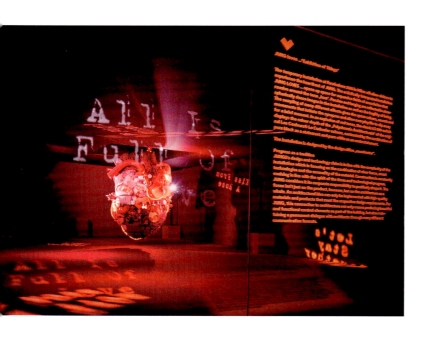

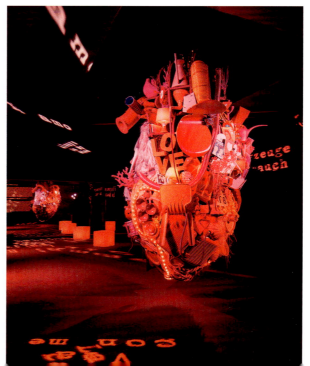

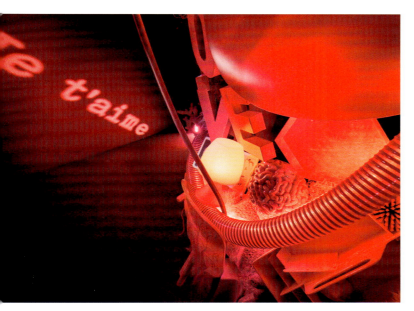

This object consisted of a pulsating heart animated by lighting effects, composed of dozens of individual objects, such as things from our childhood and youth, contemporary design objects, curiosities, oddities and esoteric items, as well as current references to architecture and interior design. A surreal and dreamlike composition.

The installation "JUNG loves" intended to show the heartbeat and longstanding dedication influencing the changes and developments at the company JUNG. The harmonised sound and light impulses sought to make the visitors' hearts beat in tune with them.

AN ARTISTIC, PULSATING SCULPTURE CONVEYS A LOVE OF ARCHITECTURE AND DESIGN.

Das dramaturgische Konzept lockte die Besuchenden zunächst mit einem tiefen Herzschlag aus dem Mailänder Sonnenlicht in die Ausstellungsfläche. Dort erwartete sie ein dunkler, magischer Raum mit pulsierenden Klängen, bewegten Textprojektionen, Farben und dem zentralen Ausstellungsobjekt.

Das Objekt bestand in einem durch Lichteffekte animierten, pulsierenden Herz, das sich aus Dutzenden von Einzelobjekten zusammensetzte. Dinge aus unserer Kindheit, unserer Jugend, Designobjekte der Gegenwart, Kuriositäten, Versponnenes und Abseitiges genauso wie aktuelle Verweise auf Architektur und Innenarchitektur. Eine surreale, traumartige Komposition.

Die Installation „JUNG loves" sollte den Herzschlag, die langjährige Leidenschaft und die dadurch beeinflussten Veränderungen und Entwicklungen der Firma JUNG spürbar machen. Die aufeinander abgestimmten Sound- und Lichtimpulse wollten den Herzschlag der Besucher:innen infizieren und im Gleichklang mitschwingen lassen.

GROHE X EXPERIENCE HUB
VOK DAMS EVENTS & LIVE MARKETING, WUPPERTAL

Location
Online; Dusseldorf (Production)

Client
Grohe Holding GmbH, Hemer

Month / Year
March 2021

Duration
Several days (Launch event), permanent (platform)

Awards
Red Dot Design Award 2021 (Digital Solutions); Honors at Galaxy Award 2021 (Event Marketing); Digital Communication Award 2021 (B2B); Silver at BrandEx Award 2022 (Best Brand Activation)

Dramaturgy / Direction / Coordination
VOK DAMS Events & Live-Marketing, Wuppertal

Architecture / Design
D'art Design Gruppe, Neuss

Others
IBM Deutschland GmbH, Stuttgart (Technology & Cloud solution)

Photos
Grohe Holding GmbH, Hemer

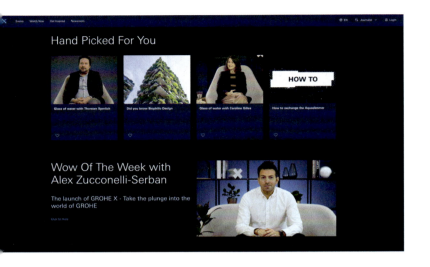

GROHE X ist eine neuartige, digitale Kommunikationsplatt-
form der Marke GROHE. Sie ging ursprünglich aus der
Online-Alternative der Offline-Messe ISH hervor und hat sich
zum dauerhaften digitalen Content-Hub für Produktpräsen-
tationen, Inspirationen und Wissenstransfer entwickelt. Mit
informativem und inspirierendem Content soll sie B2B-Inhalte
individuell erlebbar machen und das Markenerlebnis sowie
den Kundendialog auf interaktive Weise fördern.

Unter dem Slogan „Discover what's next" möchte GROHE X
ein Programm für jede Zielgruppe bieten: inhaltliche Formate, Präsentationen globaler Wohntrends, Möglichkeiten
zum Austausch mit Fachleuten, How-to-Videos, Hintergrund-
artikel sowie virtuelle 360-Grad-Räume.

A DIGITAL HUB FOR ONLINE EVENTS AND INTERACTION, AS WELL AS INFORMATIVE AND INSPIRING CONTENT.

GROHE X is a novel digital communication platform of
the brand GROHE. It developed originally from the online
alternative to the offline trade fair ISH and has become a
permanent digital content hub for product presentations,
inspiration and knowledge transfer. It is designed to enable
an individual experience of the informative and inspiring
B2B content and promote the brand experience and customer dialogue interactively.

Under the slogan "Discover what's next", GROHE X would
like to offer a programme for every target group: content
formats, presentations of global residential trends, possibilities to converse with experts, how-to videos, background
articles and virtual 360-degree spaces.

The platform was opened in March 2021. It is set up as a central hub for all communication and global marketing measures. During the opening week, there were eight live events with a total of 68,000 visitors from 140 countries. Apart from specialist events and direct communication with experts, the medium offers service-orientated options, as well as tutorials with content targeted towards international B2B mediators from trade, crafts, design and media. Creating a profile also makes it possible to personalise content and interactions according to personal requirements.

Die realisierte Plattform wurde im März 2021 eröffnet. Sie ist als zentrale Drehscheibe für die gesamte Kommunikation und alle globalen Marketingmaßnahmen angelegt. So gab es während der Startwoche acht Live-Veranstaltungen mit insgesamt 68.000 Besucher:innen aus 140 Ländern. Neben Fachveranstaltungen und dem direkten Austausch mit Expert:innen bietet das Medium serviceorientierte Angebote wie Tutorials mit auf internationale B2B-Vermittler:innen aus Handel, Handwerk, Design und Medien zugeschnittenen Inhalten. Über die Erstellung eines Profils besteht zudem die Möglichkeit, Inhalte und Interaktionen nach den eigenen Bedürfnissen zu personalisieren.

EIN DIGITALER HUB FÜR ONLINE-EVENTS, AUSTAUSCH UND INFORMATIVE WIE INSPIRIERENDE INHALTE.

Find X

thanks to an uninterrupted panorar

OPPO FIND X3 SERIES GLOBAL LAUNCH
UNIPLAN GMBH & CO. KG, COLOGNE

Location
Online / China, Toronto, State of Nebraska
(Recording)

Client
OPPO Mobile Telecommunications
Corp. Ltd., Guangdong

Month / Year
March 2021

Duration
1 day

Photos
Uniplan GmbH & Co. KG, Cologne

isplay of Find X,

Für den Smartphone-Hersteller OPPO galt es, eine Markt-einführung mit „Wow"-Moment zu schaffen. Ein Launch-Event, das den Ruf als Branchenführer festigen und über die üblichen Produkteinführungen hinausgehen sollte. Uniplan kreierte daraus die OPPO-Kampagne „Awaken Colour", die vornehmlich internationale Journalist:innen und Technik-begeisterte ansprach.

EIN DIGITALES LAUNCH-EVENT MIT FASZINIERENDEN BILDERN, FILMEN UND EINDRÜCKEN.

Das Ergebnis kombinierte die für eine Produkteinführung notwendigen technischen Informationen mit Vorträgen von Firmenvertretern: einflussreiche Kreative, die ihre Beiträge als packend erzählte Geschichten darboten. Die Präsenta-tion lud die Zuschauer:innen dazu ein, die Technologie des Produkts zu begreifen und in das Farbkonzept der neuen OPPO-Serie einzutauchen.

The smartphone manufacturer OPPO sought to create a market launch with a wow effect. A launch event that would cement their reputation as an industry leader and go beyond conventional product launches. On this basis, Uniplan created the OPPO campaign "Awaken Colour", which appealed pri-marily to international journalists and technology enthusiasts.

The result combined the technical information necessary for a product launch with presentations by company represen-tatives: influential creative minds who presented their con-tributions as stories told with excitement. The presentation invited spectators to get to grips with the product's techno-logy and to immerse themselves in the colour concept of the new OPPO series.

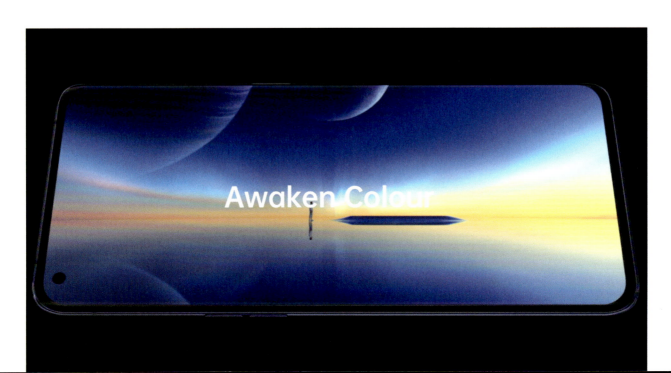

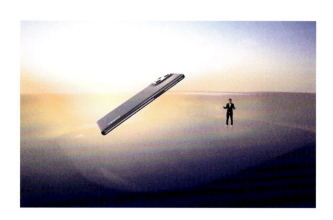

Als dokumentarisches Element wurde der Film „The Evolution of Colours" des kanadischen Dokumentarfilmregisseurs Zhang Qiaoyong integriert. Das Format wurde auf diese Weise inhaltlich aufgewertet und der Mehrwert der Technologie veranschaulicht.

Um ein möglichst mitreißendes Projekt zu realisieren, wurden internationale Partner, Regisseure und Fachleute für Extended Reality und Postproduktion hinzugezogen. So wurden die Produkte effektvoll zum Leben erweckt und dank virtuell erstellter Szenen faszinierende Inhalte erschaffen.

A DIGITAL LAUNCH EVENT WITH FASCINATING IMAGES, FILMS AND IMPRESSIONS.

The film "The Evolution of Colours" by the Canadian documentary film director Zhang Qiaoyong was integrated as a documentary element. This upgraded the format in terms of content and showed the added value of the technology.

In order to realise a project as captivating as possible, international partners, directors and specialists in extended reality and post-production were hired. This brought the products to life to great effect and, by means of virtually generated scenes, resulted in fascinating content.

BSS LOGISTREAM
KREATIV KONZEPT
AGENTUR FÜR WERBUNG GMBH, BONN

Location
Online (Livestream from two logistics centres); Geisenfeld / Papenburg

Client
BSS Bohnenberg GmbH, Solingen

Month / Year
November 2021

Duration
2 days

Dramaturgy / Architecture / Design / Graphics
Kreativ Konzept GmbH, Bonn

Direction / Coordination
Kreativ Konzept Dominik Dugandzic, Bonn

Lighting / Media
REINBLICK EVENT AGENTUR, Krefeld

Artists / Show acts
Rafael Treite, Esslingen am Neckar

Photos
Kreativ Konzept GmbH, Bonn

A LIVESTREAM AFFORDS EXCLUSIVE INSIGHTS INTO THE COMPLEX TECH- NOLOGIES OF LARGE- SCALE PLANTS.

Aufgrund der wiederholten Absage der Intralogistik-Fach-messe war die BSS Materialflussgruppe auf der Suche nach einem neuen Format, um Kunden zu erreichen und sie „up to date" zu halten. Gemeinsam mit Kreativ Konzept wurde in diesem Sinne der BSS LogiStream ins Leben gerufen: ein zweistündiger Livestream, der durch repräsentative Anla-gen führte und exklusive Einblicke ermöglichte.

Due to the repeated cancellation of the Intralogistics Trade Fair, the BSS Group was looking for a new format for reaching customers and keeping them up to date. Together with Kreativ Konzept, the BSS LogiStream was initiated with this in mind: a two-hour livestream that provided guidance through representative plants and afforded exclusive insights.

Die Projekte waren zuvor unter Ausschluss der Öffentlichkeit finalisiert worden und wurden in diesem Rahmen zum ersten Mal präsentiert. Die Ausweichveranstaltung wurde so zum wahren Mehrwert. Teilnehmer:innen gewannen exklusive Einblicke in komplexe Projekte und Technologien, die so bei einer Präsenzveranstaltung gar nicht möglich gewesen wären. Das Programm bestand aus Interviews direkt bei den Anlagen sowie gesonderten Expertentalks. Die Teilnehmenden hatten im Rahmen der Talks die Möglichkeit, individuelle Fragen zu stellen, die detailliert beantwortet wurden. Vertiefende technische Informationen bündelte eine ergänzende Landingpage.

EIN LIVESTREAM ERMÖGLICHT EXKLUSIVE EINBLICKE IN KOMPLEXE TECHNOLOGIEN VON GROSSANLAGEN.

Die enorme Größe der Anlagen und deren adäquate Abbildung waren besondere Herausforderungen. Ebenso die Vorgabe, dass der laufende Betrieb in ihnen zu keinem Zeitpunkt gestört werden durfte. Das erforderte einen sekundengenauen Ablauf, bei dem jeder Handgriff des Produktionsteams sitzen musste.

The projects had been finalised beforehand under the exclusion of the public and were presented for the first time on this occasion. The alternative event therefore offered true added value. Participants gained exclusive insights into complex projects and technologies that would not have been possible at a live event. The programme consisted of interviews directly at the plants, as well as separate expert talks. During the talks, the participants had the opportunity to ask individual questions that were answered in detail. More in-depth information was gathered on an accompanying landing page.

The huge size of the plants and portraying them suitably represented particular challenges, as well as the instruction that the ongoing operations there must not be disturbed at any point. This required planning down to the last second, whereby every action by the production team had to be on point.

Im Gegensatz zu den regulären Kategorien setzt diese Sonderkategorie einen anderen Fokus. Anstatt Zielgruppen herauszustellen, stehen die Gestalter im Mittelpunkt: der Nachwuchs.

STUDENT PROJECTS: KATEGORIEÜBERGREIFENDE SEMESTERARBEITEN UND EVENTPROJEKTE, DIE VON STUDIERENDENTEAMS UNTERSCHIEDLICHER STUDIENRICHTUNGEN KONZIPIERT WURDEN. DEM KÖNNEN DABEI SOWOHL FIKTIVE FRAGESTELLUNGEN ALS AUCH ZIELVORGABEN VON ECHTEN AUFTRAGGEBERN ZUGRUNDE LIEGEN. DIE UMSETZUNG ERFOLGT TEILWEISE IN KOMPLETTER EIGENREGIE ODER MIT UNTERSTÜTZUNG VON ERFAHRENEN FACHLEUTEN.

STUDENT PROJECTS

Contrary to the regular categories, this special category sets a different focus. Instead of focussing on target groups, the designers are at the centre: up-and-coming designers.

STUDENT PROJECTS: STUDY PROJECTS AND EVENT PROJECTS CONCEIVED BY VARIOUS FIELDS OF STUDY ACROSS DIFFERENT CATE-GORIES. THESE CAN BE BASED ON BOTH FICTIVE SUBJECT MATTERS AND SPECIFICATIONS BY REAL CLIENTS. THE REALISATION IS IN SOME CASES COMPLETELY INDEPENDENT OR ELSE WITH THE SUPPORT OF EXPERIENCED SPECIALISTS.

SCHLEMMER X BEATS
STUDIOPRODUKTION EVENT MEDIA HDM, STUTTGART

Location
Staatsgalerie Stuttgart, Sterling Hall

Client
Staatsgalerie Stuttgart

Month / Year
February 2020 (Finish: December)

Duration
1 day

Awards
Golden Nail at ADC Awards 2021; Recognition (Interaction Design) at aed neuland 2021; COMMUNICATION ARTS 2021 (Interactive / Student Work / Entertainment)

Dramaturgy
Daniel Zinser; Svetoslav Mitsev; Shari Molges

Direction / Coordination
Daniel Zinser; Julia Koken; Corbinian Pfeiffer; Sophia Schimpgen

Architecture / Design
Daniel Zinser; David Waldow; Svetoslav Mitsev

Graphics
Daniel Zinser; Sophia Schimpgen

Lighting
David Waldow; Svetoslav Mitsev

Media
Franka Bittner; Niels Keller; Markus Hirsch; Torben Rumpf

Films
Franka Bittner, Andrea Guerrero (Modelling)

Music
David Waldow; Corbinian Pfeiffer

Construction
Andrea Guerrero; Ria Goller; Torben Rumpf

Others
VISUELL Studio für Kommunikation GmbH, Stuttgart (Media planning consultation); ICT AG, Kohlberg / WIREWORX Gesellschaft für audiovisuelle Medien mbH, Stuttgart / Skyeline-live soundtechnik, Stuttgart / b&b eventtechnik GmbH, Filderstadt (Media technology)

Supervision
Prof. Ursula Drees, Stuttgart (Artistic direction); Steffen Mühlhöfer, Stuttgart (Technical direction)

Photos
Niels Keller; Ilkay Karakurt

OSKAR SCHLEMMERS TRIADISCHES BALLETT WIRD ZUR MIXED-REALITY-MUSEUMS-ERFAHRUNG.

On the occasion of the 100-year anniversary of Bauhaus, students at HdM Stuttgart were involved with a reinterpretation of the Triadic Eallet by Oskar Schlemmer. Their aim was to revive the ballet as a form of art and to create a meaningful, gamified, ocation-based and mixed-reality museum experience. The result was Schlemmer x Beats – an interactive techno art club in the Stuttgart State Gallery.

Anlässlich des 100-jährigen Bauhaus-Jubiläums befassten sich Studierende der HdM Stuttgart mit einer Neuinterpretation des Triadischen Balletts von Oskar Schlemmer. Ihr Ziel war es, das Ballett als Kunstform wiederzubeleben und eine bedeutungsvolle, gamifizierte und lokationsbasierte Mixed-Reality-Museumserfahrung zu schaffen. Das Ergebnis war Schlemmer x Beats – ein interaktiver Techno-Art-Club in der Stuttgarter Staatsgalerie.

OSKAR SCHLEMMER'S TRIADIC BALLET IS TURNED INTO A MIXED-REALITY MUSEUM EXPERIENCE.

Das außergewöhnliche Kunsterlebnis war in zwei Phasen
unterteilt: Zunächst konfigurierten Besucher:innen an „triadischen Auswahlsäulen" einen Triaden. Die mit 3D-Gips-
druck gestalteten Säulen waren Oskar Schlemmers Konzept
aus drei „Acts" und „Styles" zugeordnet: drei Stimmungen
und drei Kostümtypen. Durch Drehen der Säulen wählten
Besuchende neue Kombinationen eines triadischen Kostüms
aus. Alle trugen Bauhaus-Namen wie zum Beispiel Oskar,
Mies, Lilli, Anni oder Walter.

The unusual art experience was divided into two phases:
First of all, visitors configured a triad at "triadic selection
pillars". The pillars designed with 3D plaster printing were
dedicated to Oskar Schlemmer's concept of three "acts"
and "styles": three moods and three types of costume.
By rotating the pillars, visitors selected new combinations
of a triadic costume. All of them bore Bauhaus names such
as Oskar, Mies, Lilli, Anni or Walter.

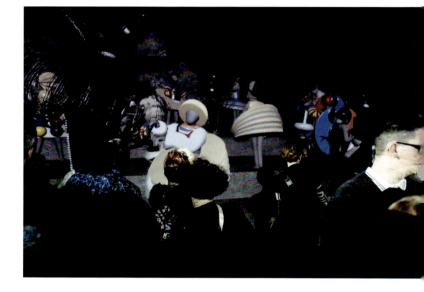

Nach der Konfiguration setzte sich die Echtzeit-Online-Projektion der Tänzer:innen im virtuellen Club fort. Besuchende und Tänzer:innen betraten den Raum. Jeder Triade erhielt „10 Seconds of Fame": Er wuchs, sein Name schwebte über dem Kopf und er zeigte besondere Bewegungen. Für diese Bewegungen wurden Schlemmers Original-Choreografien erweitert und auf Technobeats übertragen. Über Motion-Capturing-Anzüge wurden sie mit Profitänzern und -tänzerinnen digitalisiert. Dabei wurde auch die Bewegungseinschränkung durch die virtuellen Kostüme mit einbezogen.

After the configuration, the real-time online projection of the dancers in the virtual club continued. Visitors and dancers entered the room. Each triad was accorded "10 seconds of fame": It grew, its name floated over its head and it performed special movements, for which Schlemmer's original choreographies were extended and transferred to techno beats. They were digitised using professional dancers wearing motion capturing suits. The movement restriction was also incorporated through the virtual costumes.

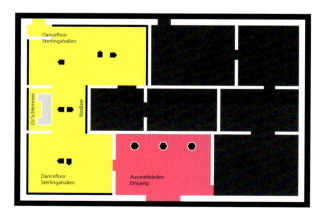

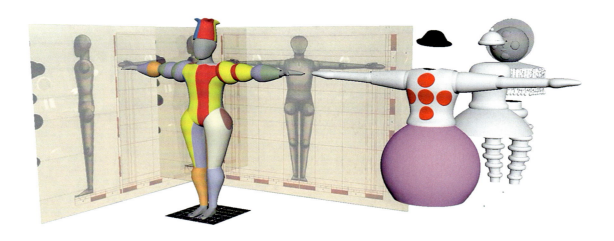

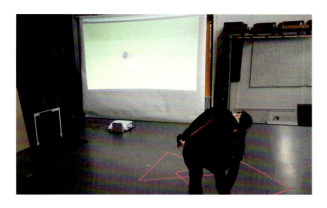

Auch die Bewegungen der DJs wurden durch Motion-Capturing-Suits aufgenommen und auf den hinter dem Pult tanzenden virtuellen „DJ Schlemmer" übertragen. Die Verteilung der Stimmungen unter den digitalen Triadischen Tänzer:innen wurde wiederum mit jeweils dazu passender Musik aufgegriffen.

The movements of the DJs were also recorded by means of motion capturing suits and transferred to the virtual "DJ Schlemmer" dancing behind the console. The range of moods among the digital triadic dancers was reflected in suitable music respectively.

DACHMOBIL
PROF. STEFAN LUPPOLD & SASKIA KRÜGER: DHBW RAVENSBURG

Locations
Various across Baden-Württemberg

Client
Landesinnungsverband des Dachdecker-handwerks Baden-Württemberg, Karlsruhe

Month / Year
November 2021 (Launch)

Duration
Ongoing (until 2026)

Architecture / Design / Graphics / Media / Decoration / Construction
vg mediastudio GmbH & Co. KG, Laichingen

Photos
vg mediastudio GmbH & Co. KG, Laichingen

Im Auftrag des Landesinnungsverbandes sollten mehr junge Menschen für das Dachdeckerhandwerk begeistert werden. Mit diesem Ziel entwickelte ein Studierendenteam des Studiengangs Messe-, Kongress- und Eventmanagement der DHBW Ravensburg ein umfassendes Konzept: von Situationsanalyse, Zielgruppenanalyse, Strategie, Marketingzielen und Maßnahmenkatalog bis hin zur Kostenkalkulation.

Herzstück der Nachwuchskampagne, die durch die Agentur vg mediastudio gmbh & co kg weiterentwickelt und umgesetzt wurde, ist ein Medienfahrzeug, das bei verschiedenen Veranstaltungen zur multimedialen Kommunikation des Dachdeckerberufs eingesetzt werden kann.

MOBILE VR ATTRAC-TIONS INSPIRE YOUNG PEOPLE TO TAKE UP THE ROOF TILING TRADE.

More young people were to be attracted to the roof tiling trade on behalf of the State Guild Association. With this aim in mind, a team of students from the Exhibition, Congress and Event Management study course at DHBW Ravensburg developed a comprehensive concept from situation analysis, target group analysis, strategy, marketing objectives and a catalogue of measures to cost calculations.

MOBILE VR-ATTRAK-TIONEN BEGEISTERN DEN NACHWUCHS FÜR DAS DACH-DECKERHANDWERK.

Das „Dachmobil" enthält drei digitale Attraktionen: Die erste ist ein VR-Game, bei dem Interessierte mithilfe von Virtual-Reality-Brillen direkt auf eine Baustelle versetzt werden. Hier können sie selbst Höhenluft schnuppern und spielerisch in mehreren Levels ihren virtuellen Kolleg:innen zur Hand gehen. Wenn das Interesse geweckt ist, informieren 360-Grad-Videos über den Berufsalltag als Dachdecker oder Dachdeckerin. Durch einen Drohnenflug-Simulator, die dritte Attraktion, präsentiert sich das Dachdeckerhandwerk schließlich als moderner Arbeitgeber, der aktuelle technologische Trends bei sich umsetzt. Diverse Kommunikationsmaßnahmen, angefangen von der Website „ObenistdasneueVorn" (https://obenistdasneuevorn.de) über Social Media bis hin zu Informationsbroschüren, begleiten das Dachmobil.

The centrepiece of the campaign targeted towards up-and-coming young roofers, which was developed further and realised by the agency vg mediastudio gmbh & co kg, is a media vehicle that can be used at various events for the multimedia communication of the roof tiling profession.

The "roof mobile" comprises three digital attractions: the first is a VR game, in which those interested are transported directly to a building site with the help of virtual reality glasses. Here they can experience what it is like to be up on a roof and playfully lend a hand to their virtual colleagues on various levels. Once their interest has been sparked, 360-degree videos provide information about the day-to-day work as a roof tiler. By means of a drone flight simulator as the third attraction, the roof tiling trade then presents itself as a modern employer that implements current technological trends. A variety of communication measures, from the website "ObenistdasneueVorn" (https://obenistdasneuevorn.de, which translates as "upwards is the new forwards") to social media and information brochures, accompany the roof mobile.

GRADUATION CELEBRATION 2021
TECHNISCHE HOCHSCHULE DEGGENDORF, MASTER STUDENTS OF MEDIA TECHNOLOGY

Location
THD Campus, Deggendorf

Client
University administration / Alumni network

Month / Year
July 2021

Duration
3 days

Dramaturgy
Hoang Kim Hong; Karolina Ottmers; Steffen Halfstad; Levke van Drathen

Direction / Coordination
Hoang Kim Hong; Steffen Halfstad

Graphics / Media
Philipp Gunkel; Calvin Reuss; Annalena Babl

Lighting
Lars Eissing

Films
Franziska Hörger; Fiona Pex; Daniel Denk; Maximilian Herici; Manuel Emrich

Music
Leo Richter

Artists / Show acts
Jakob Geissler; Lorenz Wintersperger; Maximilian Radomski (Façade projection)

Decoration
Christina Zipperer; Anna Andraschko

Catering
Studentenwerk Niederbayern / Oberpfalz, Regensburg

Construction
Lukas Lukaschik; Matthias Wolf; Lucas Ostermeier; Elisa Anthofer (Planning); Jocham Veranstaltungstechnik GmbH & Co. KG, Iggensbach (Realisation)

Others
Prof. Susanne Krebs, Maximilian Radomski (Direction of production); Lara Richter (Hygiene concept); Sandra Tremmel (Project management)

Photos
Jürgen Mayer; Johannes Schwarz

EINE GUT STRUKTURIERTE, CORONA-KONFORME ABSCHLUSSFEIER BRINGT STUDIERENDE UND CAMPUS ZUM LEUCHTEN.

Der Studienabschluss ist ein großer Moment im Leben eines jungen Menschen. Während der Pandemie konnten ihn viele Studierende leider nur eingeschränkt und ohne Familie und Freunde feiern. Die Studierenden des Masterstudiengangs Medientechnik und -produktion der Technischen Hochschule Deggendorf (THD) haben die Möglichkeiten genutzt und eine Graduiertenfeier realisiert, die die erbrachten Leistungen und Graduierten würdigte. Dabei übernahm das Team die komplette Konzeption, Planung und Umsetzung der Veranstaltung – von der Contentproduktion und Regie über Medien und Licht bis zur Fassadenprojektion.

Um alle geltenden Regelungen im Sommer 2021 einzuhalten, wurde das Event als hybride Open-Air-Veranstaltung entwickelt und auf drei Tage verteilt. Die Absolvent:innen wurden nach Fakultäten und Studiengängen sortiert und zu einem der drei Tage eingeladen. Angehörige und Freunde konnten die Graduation über einen Livestream verfolgen.

Graduation is a big moment in the life of a young person. During the pandemic, unfortunately, many students could only celebrate it in a limited manner and without family and friends. The students on the Master's course in Media Technology and Production at the Deggendorf Technical University (THD) made the most of their possibilities and realised a graduation ceremony that honoured the achievements of the graduates. The team took over the complete conceptualisation, planning and realisation of the event – from content production and direction to media and light and the façade projection.

A WELL-STRUCTURED GRADUATION CEREMONY IN LINE WITH COVID REGULATIONS MAKES STUDENTS AND THE CAMPUS LIGHT UP.

Nach dem Einlass konnten die Absolvent:innen zunächst gemeinsam anstoßen und Talar und Hut abholen. Die Übergabe der Urkunden fand in den jeweiligen Fakultäten statt und wurde live auf YouTube und Vimeo gestreamt. Mit einem persönlichen Erinnerungsfoto erhielt jeder einen „Moment of Fame", der auch live im Stream zu sehen war.

Der gemeinsame Hütewurf wurde als Höhepunkt des Abends inmitten des Campus inszeniert. Nach der Ansprache des Hochschulpräsidenten brachte eine Projektion mit über 1500 Quadratmetern bespielter Fassadenfläche in Kombination mit einer Lichtshow die Hochschule und die nun Graduierten getreu dem Motto „Glow up with us" zum Leuchten. Im Anschluss wurde bei DJ-Musik, VJ-Visuals an den Fassaden und Glow-up-Cocktails gefeiert.

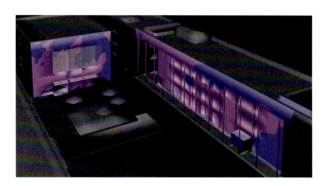

In order to comply with all the applicable regulations in summer 2021, it was developed as a hybrid open-air event and spread over three days. The graduates were divided according to faculties and courses of study and invited to one of the three days. Family and friends were able to follow the graduation through a livestream.

After being admitted, the graduates could first raise a toast to each other and collect a gown and mortar board. The handover of the certificates took place at the respective faculties and was streamed live on YouTube and Vimeo. With a personal souvenir photo, everyone was given a "moment of fame" that could also be seen live on the stream.

The throwing of mortar boards together was staged as the highlight of the evening in the middle of the campus. After the speech by the university president, a projection with an animated façade surface of over 1500 square metres in combination with a light show made the university and the new graduates light up, true to the motto "Glow up with us". Afterwards they celebrated with DJ music, VJ visuals on the façades and glow-up cocktails.

PLANTASIA
STUDIOPRODUKTION EVENT MEDIA HDM, STUTTGART

Location / Client
Zentrum für Sonnen- und Wasserstoffenergie (ZSW), Stuttgart

Month / Year
January – February 2022

Duration
18 days

Dramaturgy
Swantje Cramm; Caro Abkai; Lena Schlagenhauf

Direction / Coordination
Kim Caspers; Julija Orbitane; Sophia Walter

Architecture / Design / Decoration
Charlot Schümann; Lisa Michel; Kim Caspers; Sophia Walter; Louisa Handt

Graphics
Louisa Handt; Caro Abkai

Lighting
Isabelle Münch; Sophia Walter; Charlot Schümann

Media
Louisa Handt, Caro Abkai (AI); Isabelle Münch, Dobromir Petushev, Jürgen Popow (Media programming, technology and control)

Films
Dobromir Petushev (CA); Lisa Michel (Film, Video)

Music
Sophia Walter; Lukas Münter

Artists / Show acts
Lara Epple, Tara Seutemann, Swantje Gramm (Sponsoring, PR)

Construction
Charlot Schümann; Lisa Michel; Kim Caspers; Sophia Walter; Louisa Handt; Swantje Cramm; Caro Abkai; Lena Schlagenhauf; Lara Epple, Tara Seutemann; Jürgen Popow

Supervision
Prof. Ursula Drees, Stuttgart (Artistic direction); Steffen Mühlhöfer, Stuttgart (Technical direction)

Photos
Lisa Michel; Caro Abkai

EIN INTERAKTIVER ERLEBNISRAUM LÄSST MITHILFE VON TECHNOLOGIEN DIE NATUR SPRECHEN.

Um mehr Bewusstsein für die Natur und ihre Zerstörung durch den Menschen zu vermitteln, entwickelten Studierende aus sechs Studiengängen der HdM Stuttgart einen interaktiven Erlebnisraum: Plantasia. Er lieferte eine Interpretation zum Thema „junge Energie" und sollte bewusst machen, wie Menschen den natürlichen Lebensraum zerstören. Plantasia zeigte als bewussten Gegensatz eine unberührte, befreite, magische Naturwelt. Die Botschaft lautete: „Erlebe Natur, zerstöre sie nicht. Natur entsteht, wenn der Mensch nicht einwirkt."

In order to raise awareness of nature and its destruction by humankind, students from six study courses at HdM Stuttgart developed an interactive experience: Plantasia. It provided an interpretation of the theme "young energy" and was designed to highlight how people destroy the natural habitat. Plantasia showed a pristine, liberated, magical natural world as a pointed contrast. The message was: "Experience nature, do not destroy it. Nature is created when people do not influence it."

AN INTERACTIVE EXPERIENCE LETS NATURE SPEAK WITH THE HELP OF TECHNOLOGIES.

Plantasia führte durch drei Erlebnisphasen. Phase 1 bestand aus der Auseinandersetzung mit Umweltkräften. In einem Spiel wurde ausgetrocknete Natur durch das Sammeln von Wasser belebt. Besuchende sollten handeln. Ihre Bewegungen wurden dabei getrackt, Wasserbehälter gefüllt, Natur belebt. Die leichte Spielsystematik sprach bewusst alle Altersgruppen an. In der 2. Phase sollten die Besucher:innen der Natur zuhören. Bei der Berührung von interaktiven, echten Pflanzen entstanden Töne. Sensoren erkannten die Berührung von Blättern über die Änderung der elektromagnetischen Spannung, die wiederum in Töne bzw. Gesang umgewandelt wurde. So entstand eine Art Kommunikation. Phase 3 regte dazu an, die magische Natur zu betrachten. Eine computeranimierte Vision von Natur und vier Animationen einer durch KI erzeugten virtuellen Natur zeigten die Zukunft. Besuchende hörten Naturgeräusche aus dem Amazonas und heimischen Wäldern. Hierbei fand bewusst keine Interaktion statt, nur Betrachtung.

Plantasia guided visitors through three experience phases. Phase 1 consisted of a consideration of environmental forces. In a game, parched nature was revitalised by the collection of water. Visitors were supposed to take action. Their movements were tracked, water containers were filled and nature brought back to life. The lighthearted game method was conceived to appeal to all age groups. In phase 2, visitors were supposed to listen to nature. Sounds were emitted when touching interactive, real plants. Sensors identified the touching of leaves through the change in electromagnetic charge, which was converted in turn into sounds or singing. This resulted in a form of communication. Phase 3 encouraged the contemplation of magical nature. A computer-animated vision of nature and four animations of a virtual nature generated by artificial intelligence showed the future. Visitors heard sounds of nature from the Amazon and local forests. There was deliberately no interaction, only contemplation.

Wie schätzen Sie die Lage der Eventbranche nach der Pandemie ein? Gibt es Unterschiede zwischen den Ländern?

Es gibt Unterschiede, es gibt aber auch eine große Zahl an Gemeinsamkeiten in der Branche. Ganz unterschiedlich ist, wie die Branche während der Krise von öffentlicher Seite unterstützt wurde. In einigen Ländern, unter anderem Deutschland, wurde ein starker Fokus auf die Mitarbeiter:innen gelegt. Das Kurzarbeitergeld, wie es hier gezahlt wurde, war in Ausmaß und Länge einzigartig. Es gibt Länder, da wurden Zahlungen nur an Unternehmen gerichtet, vor allem um Mitarbeiter:innen „on the job" zu halten. Die Unternehmen haben auch die Lohnsummen vom Staat erhalten. Kanada war bei diesem Modell weit vorn. Und dann gibt es Länder, da gab es keinerlei nennenswerte Unterstützung, beispielsweise Südafrika. Was wir aktuell überall sehen: Nach zwei Jahren Stillstand gibt es einen großen Bedarf nach persönlichen Treffen.

Dies und die Absicht, möglichst viele der bisher verschobenen Veranstaltungen im Frühsommer nachzuholen, wird uns nicht von Null auf Hundert, sondern von Null auf 150 bringen.

Ein aktuell drängendes Thema ist der Personalmangel. Auch in anderen Ländern?

Ja, egal wo wir derzeit hinschauen, es gibt einen massiven Mangel an Mitarbeiter:innen. Wir merken in diesem Kontext, dass die Löhne und Gehälter anziehen und viele Firmen kooperieren, um ggf. vorhandene Lücken stopfen zu können.

Wie kann die Branche das Thema Personalmangel konkret angehen?

Wir befinden uns in einer Situation, in der viele, vor allem junge Menschen die Live-Kommunikationsbranchen nicht mehr als attraktiv wahrnehmen. Das beginnt bereits bei der Ausbildung: Hochschulen, die bisher parallele Klassen eingerichtet haben, um dem Ansturm an Studierenden gerecht zu werden, bekommen derzeit ihre Semester nicht gefüllt.

Dazu kommt, dass viele Mitarbeiter:innen, die über mehrere Monate in Kurzarbeit waren, sich andere Tätigkeitsfelder gesucht haben. Es ist offen, ob sie wieder in unsere Branche zurückkehren. Für diverse Angestellte wirken die Arbeitsplätze plötzlich nicht mehr krisenfest.

Die Lösung kann nur sein, dass wir attraktive Jobangebote schaffen. Erweiterte Möglichkeiten für Arbeiten im Homeoffice, bessere Familienverträglichkeit, aber auch höhere Löhne und Gehälter. Die Kreativbranche muss da kreativ werden. Und: Auftraggeber:innen müssen sich an steigende Kosten gewöhnen.

NICHT NUR MATERIAL IST KNAPP UND TEUER, GLEICHES GILT AUCH FÜR DIE WICHTIGSTE RESSOURCE MENSCH.

Uta Goretzky ist Executive Director bei IFES, International Federation of Exhibition and Event Services.

www.ifesnet.com

ZWISCHEN ANSTURM UND PERSONALMANGEL
BETWEEN RUSH DEMAND AND A LACK OF PERSONNEL
INTERVIEW WITH UTA GORETZKY, IFES

How would you assess the situation in the event industry after the pandemic? Are there differences between countries?

There are differences but also a lot of similarities in the industry. What differs widely is how the sector has been publicly supported during the crisis. In some countries, including Germany, a strong focus was placed on staff. The money that was paid here for reduced working hours was unique in terms of amount and duration. There are countries where payments were only directed towards companies, especially for keeping staff "on the job". The companies also received wage sums from the state. Canada was a leader by far for this model. And then there are countries where there was no support worth mentioning, for example South Africa. What we can currently observe everywhere: After a standstill for two years there is a big demand for personal meetings.

This and the intention to catch up on as many of the previously postponed events as possible in the early summer will not take us from zero to a hundred but from zero to 150.

A current urgent issue is a lack of personnel. In other countries too?

Yes, wherever we currently look, there is a huge lack of staff. We notice in this context that wages and salaries are attractive and many companies are cooperating to fill any gaps.

How can the industry tackle the issue of a lack of personnel?

We are in a situation in which many especially young people no longer perceive the live communication sectors as attractive. This already starts during education and training: Universities that previously arranged parallel classes to meet the onslaught of students can currently not fill their semesters.

In addition, many employees who had reduced working hours for several months have sought other areas of work. It remains to be seen whether they will return to our industry. For many employees, the workplaces no longer seem secure in times of crisis.

The only possible solution is to create attractive job offers. Extended possibilities for working at a home office, better compatibility with family life, as well as higher wages and salaries. The creative industry must get creative here. And: clients must get used to rising costs.

NOT ONLY IS MATERIAL SCARCE AND EXPENSIVE, THE SAME APPLIES TO PEOPLE AS THE MOST IMPORTANT RESOURCE.

Foto: Claudia Rothenberger

Uta Goretzky is Executive Director at IFES, International Federation of Exhibition and Event Services.

www.ifesnet.com

IMPRESSUM
IMPRINT

Author	Katharina Stein
Editing / Setting	Mario Ableitner
Translation	Lynne Kolar-Thompson
Layout	Tina Agard Grafik & Buchdesign, Esslingen / Neckar
Lithography	corinna rieber prepress, Marbach / Neckar
Printing	GPS Group, Villach
Paper	MAGNO VOLUME / 150 g/m^2
Cover photo	© KUNSTKRAFTWERK, 2022 / Photo: Luca Migliore Franz Fischnaller, THE GREAT CIRCLE, 2022 KUNSTKRAFTWERK Leipzig

Image recognition www.ayscan.de

avedition GmbH
Verlag für Architektur und Design
Senefelderstr. 109
70176 Stuttgart
Germany
Tel.: +49 (0)711 / 220 22 79-0
Fax: +49 (0)711 / 220 22 79-15
eventdesign@avedition.de
www.avedition.com

ISBN 978-3-89986-376-5

Redaktioneller Hinweis:
In einigen Fällen haben wir auf geschlechtsspezifische Begriffe verzichtet, um das Lesen zu vereinfachen. Falls wir die männliche Form von personenbezogenen Hauptwörtern gewählt haben, ist damit keine Herabwürdigung und / oder Diskriminierung weiblicher Personen beabsichtigt.

Deutscher Verlagspreis 22